Signing to the Angels
Claire Muller

Claire Muller          Signing to the Angels

**Cover Art:** Val Muller

**Copyright Claire Muller©2014**
**All rights reserved**
**ISBN 13:** 978-0692328156
**ISBN 10:** 0692328157

Quotes from *Le Petit Prince,* was published in 1943 by
French aristocrat, writer, poet and pioneering aviator An-
toine de Saint-Exupéry (1900-1944). (Information taken
from Wikipedia)

DWB PUBLISHING

www.dancingwithbearpublishing.com

To My Tom
Who carried My Heart
While I carried this Child.

With love to my children, Nathaniel, Shonta and Isaiah, who lived extraordinary lives, and to Laura, who became one of us.

## *P*rologue

*I*t was that 'Jesus in the Temple' thing.

It was the thing that happens to most parents at one time or another, and all we can do is remind ourselves that we are in good company because it happened to Mary and Joseph.

Early spring brought summer heat to the Sunday, as we drove home from church. I was thinking about getting out of dress-up clothes, and Tom was thinking about the clunking sound vibrating from our van.

After helping Shelly, who was seven years old at the time, out of her seat, I let her play around the yard and van with the other kids, who were reluctant to leave the beautiful day to go into the house. Tom thought he could stay out and make a few adjustments on the vehicle without getting dirty, so I ran inside to put on shorts. It took a few minutes to locate my summer clothes and change. Afterwards I went out to determine if tuna sandwiches, our regular Sunday lunch, would be okay with Tom. I found him still engaged in the mysteries of guys, expecting to come to terms with this clunking noise, and do it before the problem's cost exceeded the original cost of the van.

"So where did Shelly poke off to?" I asked.

He gave me the beginnings of a wary look. "She went inside with you—I thought."

"I left her playing here by the van when I went in to change. I thought you knew it." My voice was shrill.

Mary must have had the same disbelief in her voice when she confronted Joseph, though I am thankful that I didn't have anyone universally important to the worlds' salvation to start searching for. We felt bad enough as it was, beginning to walk around the yard, which is surrounded in a vague sort of way with black plank horse fencing. We did not catch any sign of Shelly.

When you search for a deaf-blind child, it is different from any other 'kid search'. You don't bother to yell her name. You look in the unlikely places, such as near the compost pile. Shelly has, in the past, wandered briefly into the woods surrounding our home, where branches can be a threat.  Once she strayed into the field of tall grass and cattle on our rented hundred acres. So, immediately, all of our children, without the excuse of a wheelchair, were dispatched to these areas.

I was about to check the fields myself, when I saw an awful look come over Tom's face. It seemed impossible to think about, but all the way down our long and winding driveway, and not far from the road, is the bridge, with no sides and the water up high on this early spring day. As soon as the thought struck him, Tom took off. I have never seen him run so fast; he may never have done so. Like a crazy person, he raced through the field alongside the drive and out of my sight.

I caught up visually with him at the bend of the drive, my heart still believing it was impossible for Shelly to have gone so far in such a short time. Tom crossed the bridge and barely caught up with Shell, only two or three feet before she stepped into the busy, blind curve of the road. I watched as he touched her arm and she happily turned to him; without any fuss, took his hand and let him lead her back on the long walk home.

They crossed the bridge, water rushing in torrents below, and the worn out guardian angels sitting on the edges in well-deserved rest. I imprinted the sight of her in my mind—her soft green dress and sneakers, her amazingly deep red hair, thick and flowing past her waist, her innocent, happy face upturned in the warm breeze, and her brave, jaunty walk.

Tom said nothing to Shell. She couldn't have heard

the things another child would have heard: "You scared us to death. Don't you know you could have been killed?" All the things an anxious parent blurts out in fear.

She couldn't see the cars, or the water, or the fright on our faces. She was totally and immeasurably innocent. She *felt* the world. It was good, and she went out to embrace it.

> "The best and most beautiful things in
> the world cannot be seen or even touched.
> They must be felt within the heart."
> (Helen Keller)

~ *One* ~

*If* only we could get through life unscathed. That would be our wish—to be spared a huge loss—an over-whelming pain—a crisis with results which stop our world from its normal rotation and make us change, make us face who we are, and what we believe.

We don't want to change with drama. We want to change on our own terms and slowly, imperceptibly. We fear death sometimes, but to stay sane we put the inevitable out of our minds.

We also fear being singled out for depth. Depth is not inevitable so we'd like to skirt around it whenever possible. The local news reports a car crash in our town and we listen for the names of those involved. The empathy we feel for the victim comes only fast on the heels of the momentary relief when it is no one we know.

If we know them distantly, we have sorrow for others combined with knowledge-status. We can tell someone about the accident with a more 'first-hand' knowledge: *It was the sister of a boy in my class. It was a friend of my babysitter.* When we know them better, we hurt more. When we know them very well, we hurt very much.

No one wants to hear their doctor say, "It's cancer." We want to walk out of his office with a 'free ticket' in our hands—it is benign—it is a fluid cyst—it is nothing to worry about. We never want to know what chemo feels like, what surgery feels like, or what waiting for results feels like.

We want to give birth to children without defects and we don't want to know the inner workings of Early Childhood Development, types of leg casts or how to pronounce Myelo-meningocele.

We want to wake to food in the refrigerator of a House that didn't burn down overnight, to send our kids off to a school that won't be targeted by a gunman, to go to work without facing a pink slip, to come home without finding an ambulance in our driveway, to read books to our sighted and hearing children before bed, to relax in front of our favorite show, undisturbed by a 9/11 call, and we want to get up the next day, rinse and repeat.

We're not asking for much, are we? Not much growth there, but it works—day to day in relative peace and harmony, considering the possibilities.

I am not an explorer, you say. I don't fly the heavens toward distant planets or care what lies along the Nile. I can see the ocean well enough from the surface. No, I am not an explorer. But the least explored is within us.

I'd not lose what I found there for 'normal' again.

How many times would I phone Tom at work, hold a regular conversation to see how the wind blew in his universe, and then say something to the effect of, "He's tiny, three years old, on a heart monitor, afraid of men." Or, "She has Downs Syndrome, heart problems, and needs surgery soon." Or, "She's 15, pregnant, abused, and having some trouble in school." Whatever strange thing I would blurt out, Tom's answer was almost always the same. "Okay, and when are they coming?"

He would laugh, because of the rampant chaos of our lives. We never found ourselves asking God with each child if this is what he wants us to do. We figured he'd not have sent the kid our way if it wasn't what he wanted us to do. We figured he would have mentioned in scriptures if taking in and loving some new kid was against his will. Sometimes we needed to say no for one good reason or another, but mostly we just welcomed the chaos and God didn't seem to mind.

So it was, when Vicky joined our family.

I called Tom to explain. "She's three months old, has something called *Microcephaly*, as well as an incomplete brain stem. She also suffers from seizures and I'll need to get some training at the hospital before they release her."

"When does she come?" was all he asked.

In less than four sweet years of life, Vicky taught us much. She was our first medically fragile child, although we had several with special needs. We became familiar with all types of seizures, as Vic had many every day and throughout the night. We learned how to hook up heart monitors, oxygen machines, and G-tubes. We would sit comfortably talking, with her across our lap, pounding her back with a soft plastic 'whacker' to break up the mucus in her lungs.

CPR became second nature to us and with my lips to her forehead I could quite accurately gauge her fever. Often up to eight times a night we would waken when she simply stopped breathing, which sounded an invisible alarm more rousing than a screeching wail could be. We could jump from our bed to her crib-side, start up her suction machine, clear her airways, perform CPR if necessary, return to bed and fall right back into much needed sleep until she woke us again.

Once, while staying with another child in the hospital, Tom rushed Vicky, who had aspirated fluid into her lungs, to another nearby hospital. First, he needed to drop off our other two kids with a friend, but pulled over en route, squeezing between several car seats, revived Vicky with CPR and returned to driving while calmly answering questions posed by the verbal kids.

Though she never spoke, Vicky would smile and laugh, often at nothing discernible. She never passed the twenty pound mark and still managed to look happily plump. With no muscle tone to speak of, she lay like a babe-in-arms, content with the world or quietly sick.

A year after Vicky died and I could look at her things and pictures without bursting into tears, we got a phone call from the nurse who oversaw Kentucky's foster children.

Estelline's down-to-earth, frank manner could be off-setting, or remarkably refreshing. Years later, after the death of another of our medically fragile children, Whitney, she looked at me, anxious to place yet another child.

"So, how long do you need to grieve?" she asked.

This time, Estelline was calling to set up a meeting about a child and would give very little information over the phone. Perhaps she felt she would succeed best with a face-to-face appeal. She asked to meet the following Saturday, but Tom was working and it was the day our sons, Nathaniel and Isaiah, and our daughter, Shonta, took violin lessons in Lexington.

"Perfect!" she said. "I can meet you after your lessons at the fast food place on Alumni Drive."
Estelline beat us there and I felt her watching eyes as we pulled into a parking space. I managed Shonta slowly inside with her walker and leg braces, and got Isaiah, my happy-two year-old, strapped into a high chair. I bought them a drink to go with their animal crackers and allowed Nathan, mature in his six years, be 'in charge' at the table next to ours.

For years I kept the scrap of paper with the notes from that meeting. Estelline did her best to describe Michelle and her situation to me but the more she spoke, relaying what she knew from Shelly's doctors and nurses, the more confusing my notes seemed to get.

There wasn't a doubt in my mind or Tom's. We would take this little redhead, if God kept the doors open to do so. But obviously, it would take a lot of training to prepare for her, and thus, time away from our children. We decided to trust God with the details and said, "Yes."

The world shifts...

11

## ~ *Two* ~

*It is only with the heart that one can see rightly;*
*what is essential is invisible to the eye.*
*(Le Petit Prince)*

*W*hat we were first told by the nurses who loved her: Michelle - Shelley - Shelly - Shell.

She was deaf and blind—she had amazing senses.
She was passive—she had a wicked temper.
She loved people—she pushed people away.
She was smart—she knew very little of anything.
She was chaotic—she insisted on routine.
She was happy—she was angry.
She was weak—she was strong as an ox.

They said it might take a team of aides to hold her for a procedure, but it would take only a single shift to fall in love with her forever.
What we were first told by the doctors who loved her:
They said, "Michelle was extremely complicated".
They said, "Her primary difficulties were with a secretory diarrhea of unknown etiology".
They said, "She has multiple procedures for venous access and Nissen fundoplication and tube gastrostomy, reduction of interception, numerous complications from her therapy. Also of note (in review of her systems) were bilateral blindness, bilateral deafness and a pseudo-obstruction, or a dysmotility pattern, and whether this represents her primary disorder or not, is unclear."
And they said, "Shelly continues to humble us."
We soon came to realize that both the nurses and

the doctors pretty much nailed her down... Michelle was an enigma.

*~ Stacey Overturf, Nurse ~*
*"What can I say about Michelle? Some of the other nurses called her Shelly, but for some reason, she is Michelle to me. As a brand new nurse, Michelle was my very first patient. Fresh out of nursing school, opening a new unit at Children's Hospital, nervous about who would be my first patient. Her bright red hair was the first thing everyone saw. I was immediately in love. She seemed like a normal ten month old, until I found out she was blind and she didn't talk. How was I going to communicate with this little creature?*

*I quickly found she had her own way of communicating. She cooed and whined and made her presence known. She learned quickly how to differentiate between nurses. Earrings! I wore small pearl earrings. The first thing she did when I put her side-rails down was crawl over and reach up to feel my ears. Working full-time, she quickly recognized those pearl earrings—she would then smile, and let me hold her.*

*I knew this was where I was supposed to be. If there had been any doubt, there wasn't now. We were not supposed to get attached to patients—be professional, be detached. But this little girl had no family with her. Her biological family lived in Kentucky and didn't have the resources to visit very often. We became her family. I became her family.*

*It was my first experience at being a mom. And of course, I only took care of her 8-10 hours a day, five days a week, but I felt like a surrogate mom. I loved her like I would my own; felt her pain, rejoiced in her accomplishments, and wished for her a life of abundant joy. But there were times I needed to be professional, a little distant, because there were necessary procedures to be per-*

13

*formed, tests to do, needles to be stuck, things a mother would want to protect their child from. As her nurse, I had to do these things, but I was always there afterward for the loving hugs. To hold and to comfort. She became part of my family. As much as she needed me, I needed her.*

*After over a year and little involvement from her family, a foster family in Kentucky was found and the mother planned to come meet Michelle. Having been her "mother" for over a year, I felt a little—no a lot—threatened by this woman wanting to come and take Michelle away from me—like she could do a better job.*

*She wasn't a nurse, she knew nothing about Michelle. No one asked me. But when I met Claire, she was so caring, so humble, so willing to learn. She immediately fell in love with Michelle just like I did. I didn't want to like her but I did.*

*Now, how can I teach her everything I know about Michelle? About her likes, her dislikes, how she likes to be held, how to take care of her medical needs, how to give her the love I have given her over this last year? Claire didn't need any help with the love part. She overflowed with love for Michelle and for me. Although very sad, I felt at peace in letting Michelle start a new life, sure to be filled with abundant joy."*

## ~ *Three* ~

*"Are you looking for chickens?"*
*"No," said the Little Prince. "I am looking for friends.*
*What does that mean, to tame?"*
*"It is an act too often neglected," the fox said. "It means*
*to establish ties."*
*(Le Petit Prince)*

*I* arrived for the first time at *Columbus Children's Hospital* on a cold January day, not knowing where to go or who to see. A small woman with short, almost spiky, red hair saw my lost look and hurried over to ask if I came about Michelle. Relieved to have been found so quickly, I followed her to an admitting room to get the first of the many pink *PARENT* badges I would sport over the next 16 years.

Sharon Cogan, my red-haired guide, worked for the hospital in social services, and became a beloved person along my Shelly journey. Sharon had been trying to contact me at home to warn me of a setback Shell experienced the night before and thus wouldn't be able to leave the hospital any time soon. I didn't mind having come, since I could at least meet my new child. Perhaps I was a bit relieved to take things more slowly.

Shelly had an *episode* the night before, and spiked a fever, which soon proved to be a septic line. I was anxious to go into her room but Sharon almost physically held me back, wanting to brace me for the first sight of a child hooked up with wires like tentacles reaching out to different machines surrounding her.

*What hideous thing is in the room beyond?* I wondered, and finally gently pushed my way in. I smiled. Far from frightening, the steady hum of technology comforted

15

me. The wired up child before me, blanket kicked aside, asleep and pale, reminded me right away of Vicky. Hospitals were familiar places to me by then and I found the sights and sounds reassuring. Still, Sharon kept taking my arm and watching my face for signs of a possible faint, I suppose, asking me if I was okay. Her concern for my reaction would have made me laugh, if I didn't think I would hurt her feelings. Perhaps the fear of losing a prospective parent for this hard-to-place child made her cautious.

I spent the afternoon becoming familiar with Shelly's doctors, nurses, and the hospital. I asked all the questions I wanted and got a rudimentary education of her needs; being scrutinized by her nurses let me know how much she was loved and protected. It was very late when I was finally alone with her for the first time and could think quietly.

Devastatingly ill, it would, in fact, be another two months before Shelly would be released to go home with me. I touched her short red hair, so recently growing back from a spell of total loss. Apparently when the body desperately needs nutrients, the unimportant things like hair are the last to get served.

With the room lights dimmed and time alone with my thoughts, I stayed up all night, watching Shelly sleep. In her small helplessness, she looked so much like my Vicky. Exhausted from the long day, I had trouble separating the two in my mind. That night I grieved for Vicky with a sadness I thought far behind me, and finally said goodbye to her fragile sweet life. The next morning, my eyes could see only Shelly, unique in the world—claiming my heart.


*~ Patti Kegle, Nurse ~*
*"I took care of Michelle from infancy until the day she was blessed to go home with you!*

*I have so many memories of her. I honestly believe she made me the nurse I am today. Caring for her was not a job—it was a true honor. I remember the days leading up to the day you met her—I remember all of us saying, "No one is going to be able to take care of Shelly the way we did."*

*We convinced ourselves that whoever walked through the door to take her away was not going to be good enough for Shelly. Then (and I am not exaggerating one bit) you walked in and peace washed over all of us. Of course we were going to miss our Shelly but somehow, we just KNEW she was supposed to be with you guys, she was going home, she was going to be safe and loved and what more could we have asked for?"*

The nurses scrutinized me from the moment I got to Columbus Children's. I didn't blame them. Michelle had been their little girl for two and a half years, and they knew her better than anyone, so of course, they guarded her and wanted the best for her. If they didn't approve of me, I expect they would have raised an alarm.

So many nurses cared for her, but Stacey was the one I was really taking Shelly away from. Michelle had been Stacey's first 'charge', and they were together for a long time. Impossible idea in her life right then, but she dearly wanted to become Shell's foster mom.

The tears at parting time flowed freely as all of us lingered in the hallway of 5-Tower South, passing Shelly around. She wore a new outfit bought by a loving nurse that morning.

How hard it was to just carry this innocent child out with me, as if I knew what I was doing! A huge sense of re-sponsibility suddenly overwhelmed me. I began to realize how all these trained, loving, experienced people who had been taking care of this fragile child all this time, day in and day out, shift after shift, would rightly expect me to carry on, nurse her illnesses and keep her alive. They Would also rightly expect me to teach her to walk, get educated, love her constantly, and make her happy. I began to realize my own shift would be a long one.

Stacey drove us to the airport. I felt terrible for her and hoped we would become friends somehow. I wanted to give her something to thank her and to remember the day with, so I ducked into a shop at the airport and got a small flower in a vase. Gracious and sad, hopeful and worried, Stacey waved to us as we boarded the plane.

That day wove Stacey into our lives. She married and was blessed with three beautiful girls, but I suspect she always held a place for Shell as a 'first' child. I spent many hours with her on subsequent hospital trips and visited her home. There were many phone calls in those early times that I knew only Stacey and Shelly's other nurses would have the answers for.

Another person entered our lives on the day I brought Shelly home, tangled up in the heartstrings of this redheaded child.

I saw a man on the outskirts of the action, as we grouped together outside for final goodbyes. Nice looking, quietly observant, he appeared obviously interested, though he held himself back from the rest. I wondered to myself how he was tied to Michelle.

Occasionally, in life, you see someone and feel an immediate connection. I felt it with him right then so I was disappointed when I found myself unable to figure him out before we left for home.

Just as we finished buckling Shell into the car seat, I felt a hand on my arm and turned see the man beside me. He slightly bowed, as if not wanting to take up too much space or too much of my time, and he spoke quietly. "I just wanted to wish you the best with Michelle, and I'm happy to see she is going to get a good home." I thanked him and asked him for his name, but he only said he was not important and he just wanted to wish us well.

That was my introduction to *Columbus Don*... No introduction at all. And yet, the circle of Shell's life would hold him most treasured.

~ *Four* ~

Shell came to us in mid-March of 1988, trying life without her Broviac.

A Broviac, like a Hickman, is a soft silicone IV catheter which goes to a central vein, usually in the neck, upper chest or groin. It's tunneled under the skin and brought out on the chest or thigh away from the site where it enters the vein. Hopefully, this keeps bacteria away from the central portion of the catheter, lessening the occurrences of staph infection. There is a thicker 'cuff' of silicone which is under the skin, allowing body tissue to adhere, making the 'line' more stable.

One of Shelly's main problems was the inability to absorb the nutrients and calories she needed through her 'gut'. Eating food, like the rest of us, wouldn't keep her from starving, and nutrition coming in through the veins, by-passed that problem.

Each 'line' was placed in surgery, so each line was a big deal. A lot of work was put into keeping the Broviac stable and when you're dealing with children, to whom normalcy itself includes chaos, it's an interesting exercise in parenting to keep one in place for very long. This, I believe, is especially true when it involves a stubborn, fearless deaf/blind child, like Michelle.

Children receive Broviacs when they need long term IV nutrition for various medical reasons. It keeps them from being poked again and again, and many children, like Shelly, assume it as a normal part of their lives.

The IV line is hooked up for a specified length of time to a bag of TPN, or Total Parenteral Nutrition. Basically, this is a bag of "perfect" food, imperfectly given. A nutritionist can concoct a potion specifically for a person's

needs, including sugars, carbs, proteins, fats (also called
*lipids*), electrolytes and some trace elements. Other addi-
tions, like vitamins and the blood thinner, heparin, may be
added to the bag just before infusing.

By the time I met Shelly, all the veins below her
waist had been used up in her first two and a half years.
Veins become scarred from use and block the flow of
blood, and when staph infections weaken an area, you may
just run out of placements. Since then, all her lines have
been in the chest area.

Our family pediatrician, Dr. Ron, always pointed out
that having an IV in the body is an unnatural addition and
the body is going to want to reject it eventually.

At the time of her homecoming, we hoped Shell
would not need IV's anymore, and could rely on her G-tube
until she learned to eat by mouth, an ability one is capable
of losing from lack of use.

A G-tube is a device, surgically inserted directly into
the stomach through the stomach wall, to give direct feedings from a syringe (bolus feeds) or over a period of several
hours with a drip, measured by a user-friendly machine.

Naturally, since the G-tube didn't require going
through the veins, it appeared to be a safer prospect than
life on a Broviac. They were having fairly good success with
G-tube feeds for a couple months before they dismissed
Shell from Children's Hospital. Because of Vicky, I was very
familiar with G-tubes, so I was confident of making Shell's
nutrition program proceed as planned.

Shelly never does anything according to plan. This
truth was the first and most consistent thing Shell taught
me, her doctors, teachers and therapists about herself—
Shelly *never* does anything according to plan.

With some ups and downs, the G-tube feeding began
just fine. She came to us in March and not only did we have
experience with this kind of feeding, but we could work
with the doctors over the phone to make adjustments. For

a couple of months we alternated pushing the formula in at once with bolus feeding, and the 24-hour a day hook-ups, trying to find the right mix.

Then the diarrhea started.

It began as an off-and-on again struggle but Shell's body seemed to rebel and daily the amount of unbelievable poop increased, first filling her diapers, then leaking out to fill the sheets, the bed, and the floor beneath her crib. As fast as I could turn around I would be changing, changing, and changing.

When I look back now, my thought on that time is, "Lord, help us, we didn't even know about disposable gloves. We could have been using *disposable gloves*." We could scrub ourselves 'clean' but never seem to be free from the awful smell in our clothes, skin, hair, and home.

Her doctors decided we should make the switch from bolus feedings to continuous feeds, and Shell began getting a slow drip of food 24-hours a day. Nothing helped and the diarrhea grew worse.

I started keeping paper plates nearby, and would rip one in half to have two scoopers for filling plastic garbage bags, or use paper cups to ladle it while holding my breath—so acidic, it made my eyes water. Starvation diarrhea is what I came to think of it because it appeared she could starve even as she was being constantly fed. Her arms and legs growing thinner as her belly extended, resembling the children from Biafra.

About the middle of June, I took her back to Children's Hospital feeling defeated. All of our early expectations had been high for Shell to live a life free of IV's. We were sure she could eventually learn how to eat normally. Wasn't her deafness and blindness a challenge enough for any child? I returned home to care for my other children, leaving her in the best hands with her first family.

I believe the first effort at the hospital was to keep

trying her G-Tube—they didn't know me very well yet, and must have wondered what I did wrong. Soon they realized there was no choice but to find a vein and resume her broviac feedings. Shell was promising to be one for the books.

## ~ *Five* ~

*It is the time that you have lost for your rose that*
*makes your rose so important.*
*(Le Petit Prince)*

Shell had been hospitalized almost two months
when I headed back to Ohio Childrens' to learn how to hook
up an IV. I went with one thing in mind: Learn fast.

I left my other kids at home with Tom for the days it
would take to make this new knowledge stick to my scattered brain cells, and I figured the quicker, the better.

If there could have been a more naïve mindset than
the one I brought to the hospital that day, it deserves to be
in the record books. Anyone with better judgment, and a
natural sense of self-preservation would have fled in another direction. It wasn't a noble trait getting me started,
or profound wisdom keeping me going. It was pure simple-
mindedness.

If I had a lick of logical fear, I would have reasoned
several things out along the way. For one thing, my life
lacks structure. I'm not a structured person by nature, and
structure, lots of structure, is almost demanded by the situation. I say 'almost' because we've all made it this far, so
you can apparently do without. Nevertheless, the real candidate for this job is a structured person. Unfortunately,
the real candidate never showed up.

Another thing I should have reasoned out before
starting, if I was a 'reasoning out' kind of person, would be
the germ factor. Naturally, (she laughed later, much
later...) taking a child out of a presumably sterile-ish environment of a hospital, where said child lived continuously
for the first full twenty-eight months of her life, and plunk-
ing the sterile-ish child smack dab in the center of random

fertile germs, coming from random germy new brothers and sisters, random germy dogs and cats, grass, dirt and other random germy nature, well, it's just not *done!* Not done at all.

I should have felt the need for nurse's training. I should have felt the need for a better grasp of math, chemistry, and biology—or any grasp at all. But not me. I just wanted to learn what I needed to know and get home to the rest of the gang with my little redhead.

So, I went in with a "Name That Tune" attitude. The normal training time is three days or until comfortable working with IV's, and the doctors and nurses were comfortable with what was learned. So, my thought was: I can learn it all in two days, tops. Maybe a day and a half. *Name That Tune!*

I started with the reading material they gave me. I read every word, circled unfamiliar words to ask about, and stayed up most of the night memorizing the concepts and steps, the safety measures and indications. I reviewed every way I could possibly infect the line and how to keep the procedure sterile. I learned the appropriate reaction to infection, blockage, tears in the broviac, and fever spikes.

During and after the paperwork study, I asked everyone who came into the room every question imaginable. I hounded them for answers to anything I could conceive of happening and they told me of things I couldn't ever imagine happening. Thus began my introduction to 'truth is truly stranger than fiction.'

I still wasn't bright enough to be worried. I was quite sure I could retain the main event, read my trusty paperwork for the details, and make a call to 5-Tower South nurses if I needed to. Little did I know how soon I would memorize the number of 5-Tower South.

The hospital's nutrition guru, Becky Menning (soon to be Becky Hoagland), instantly became my mentor and I tagged after her in the halls on the first day making a completely tiresome companion of myself; pestering her for answers, asking for her at every spare moment to observe my hands-on attempts and at the end of the day, being shocked when she pronounced me 'ready to go'! Suddenly I felt a bit inadequate. They gave me the chance to do the hook-up myself that evening, and again in the morning before releasing Shelly to go home.

I felt like a first time skydiver, whose instructor only casually mentions where the rip-cord is before he jumps from the plane. But actually, the amazing staff at Columbus Children's Hospital is accustomed to sending children home, who will be on all sorts of devices. They know how to train the unsure moms and dads, aware there will be questions from the moment they start their solo flight.

They tirelessly answer questions already covered in training, because they know it all looks different in the hospital, and when you get home you can forget everything. Where then are the guiding nurses, you wonder? Where are the clean sheets and shiny rails of a hospital bed, with the equipment all set out before you in orderly array?

I got home in mid-afternoon and felt no immediate worries, getting Shelly settled back in and catching up on hugs from the other kids. A phone call from a place named Caremark brought me back to a necessary sense of responsibility. "Mark," the driver from Caremark, called to be sure he had the right directions to our house. Yes, it's the old haunted looking house he had already passed and wondered about. He soon pulled into the driveway, the first of many times and of many years of delivering supplies, soon becoming a beloved member of our Shelly-connected family.

When the huge piles of boxes arrived that first afternoon, reality hit hard and fast. It dawned on me how late in the day it was, and I would need to hook her IV up soon if she were to be on the twelve-hour-a-night schedule of being infused. I had no idea where to start, and was embarrassed to admit to my husband just how clueless I felt. After all, he'd just stayed home for two days caring for the other kids, assuming I would return well-trained.

I attempted to 'look smart' as my dad would say. I opened a couple boxes and tried to picture their contents in the hospital setting. The hospital is hopelessly far removed from my crazy home setting, so I tried looking at my paperwork again. I actually blushed from embarrassment, and got more and more flustered. It all seemed so impossible! In the meantime, Shelly needed constant attention, so I was distracted beyond any concentration. I finally gave her to Tom to amuse elsewhere, thus removing them both from my baffled presence. I'd rather feel stupid alone.

Thus alone, I found myself beginning at the end several times. I repackaged the boxes of scattered equipment when I realized I was just placing things around willy-nilly. Then I got a table near Shelly's bed cleared and cleaned, as well as fresh sheets on her bed. I found the blue pump, pre-set for the time and amount, and figured out how to hang it on its long metal pole. Whenever Tom passed the door of the room, bouncing Shelly in his arms, I would make myself look busy and official about the business at hand, actually posing with a syringe or a pen over my paperwork.

Thank goodness IV supplies all come in sterile packaging. I rummaged through boxes, taking out and sorting, manhandling everything in hopes something would seem familiar. It was becoming a nightmare.

I finally found what I needed the most—the phone number to the nurses' station at 5-Tower South. I called and got Char, who was long familiar with every aspect of this child she helped to raise. She must have been quietly laughing, while she helped me sort things out. Slowly I proceeded to the point that Shelly herself became necessary to the process, and Tom brought her in for me. He must have wondered if every night was going to take as long as the first.

Like any new skill, time and experience are the only way to be comfortable with it all. In the following days I got the boxes of supplies sorted and could find the needle sizes I needed, as well as the big and little bottles, sterile and non-sterile gloves, surgical and non-surgical padding, long and short tubing.

Eventually, it all became second nature. I learned to stop when something seemed "off" to me and re-evaluate my process, because the sense of being "off" meant some mistake was indeed in the making. If I was distracted and found myself with a 5 cc syringe in one hand and a heparin bottle in the other, and feeling "off", I'd just stay still and think for a moment. I would be holding either the wrong bottle or the wrong syringe.

Totally exhausted, I slept poorly that first night. The new fears I now faced were real and life-threatening—fears of septic lines, air bubbles, incorrect meds, and a host of other problems I'd not known existed before I blithely boarded the plane just 3 days earlier to get trained.

The thing I knew least of all: the heart of this child and my own would soon be linked closer than any IV could connect. Her scars would become as imprints on my essence, her fevers would spike a rise in my own pulse, and soon I would see far past the physical to her dear, uninjured spirit.

~ *Six* ~

*So* Shelly was ours. Not exactly like bringing a new-born home from the hospital, of course, but in many areas everything was new. Except for one trip to a hairstylist with her nurse, Stacey, Shell had never left the Children's Hospital for her first two and a half years. We had the world to show her.

Walking was an unlearned skill. She could walk by holding a nurses' hands, but had never ventured out alone. Her balance was later considered legendary, but at the time she came to us she was lost in space. Holding her was a joy, and seemed safer and easier, so we all had to remind ourselves that she needed to be independent.

Our son, Nathan, was six years old and proudly helped by leading and lightly letting go of her hand for moments at a time, reaching in to reassure her he was still there. He was learning early to see things through blind eyes, and would often close his own and try to make it around the house.

Our son, Isaiah, was three days younger than Shelly and became a bit of a measuring rod for us to judge Shelly's progress. If he could walk and run, then we should expect, on good-feeling days that Shell might do the same. Her hands explored his play, as he rode the large bouncy horse we kept in the house, and emulating, was soon spending hours happily "riding" on her own, head thrown back, laughing in delight.

Our daughter, Shonta, was out of braces by then and enjoying more liberty with a wheelchair. Shell would hold the handles and "push" Shonta through the house, her legs getting stronger with use.

Imagine not seeing—not hearing. How do you learn to read? If you are deaf, you see the letters. If you are blind,

29

you hear the letter-sounds to learn Braille.

The more you think about the difficulties, the more difficulties you think about. And if, like Principessa, your world is so small... The picture book of an elephant shows a deaf child an elephant. A vivid storyteller shows a blind child an elephant, but where Shell is, there are no elephants.

Perhaps at a zoo, you may say. True, we could find days she would be well enough for the hour or more drive to a zoo, allowing her to feel an elephant, or even ride an elephant, but then we've only covered the elephants, right? Can she touch a swan, a deer, an eagle, a snake, a mouse, a giraffe and a rat?

And that's just touching animals. They won't make sense to her without learning where they live--touch the jungle? Touch the desert? Touch the sky? How many "feeling well" days do you have, Sweet Bean?

*I would tell you of the moon—I would tell you of the stars. I would tell you of the ocean depths and the mountains high. I would tell you fish swim, monkeys screech, and bats come out at night and you do know night. Right?*

*I would tell you about volcanoes and lightning and islands. I would tell you of mysteries—women in high heels, men in suits, and teen-aged boys with their pants half down.*

*I would tell you about nations, without telling you of wars. I would tell you about cities without telling you of crime. I would tell you about promises, without telling you of lies. I would tell you about families without telling you of feuds. I would tell you about salvation, without telling you of sin.*

Ah, you got me there, Shell—your turn—tell me.

Some things I would never tell you...

I would never tell you laughing out loud in most

public places is never done in finer circles, or when you are tired of someone, you can't just sign to them 'good-bye' and expect them to leave, or climbing into your Mama's lap when you feel hurt or sad or lonely or happy is not age appropriate. Some things I'll never tell you.

## ~ *Seven* ~

*I* think MaryLayne, our first social worker, was old before my birth, old when we first met, and old when I last saw her, but she never aged a bit in all the time I knew her. Always the same slow-moving dependability, her raspy voice evaluating the situation with us, she doggedly filled out her paperwork in shorthand. MaryLayne could take fast notes, but could never read her notes later. So she would phone us late into the night and we'd discuss all we had already gone over during the day, trying to decode the script.

There was something terribly brave about Mary-Layne, as if surrounded by a protective barrier normally bestowed on innocents. We would hear stories of her arriving at the doorstep of a family needing to have children removed and not waiting for the police to escort her through the process. She felt the police would frighten the children. Families are very often, and understandably, upset when a worker arrives with paper authority to remove a child, even if it is obviously warranted. There can be a real threat of violence, but MaryLayne never seemed to notice. She had no malice and absolutely no tendency to be condescending, so I suppose she was protected by her lack of guile.

I worried about her safety when we'd finish on the phone and realize it was almost midnight. Several times I insisted she stay inside until Tom could drive downtown and walk her to her car, but most nights she would leave the ancient social services building alone and slowly make her way through the poorly lit parking lot to her old boat of a car, driving home without a thought of muggings or carjackings. She seemed to think the best about the world when every day her job brought her reasons to think the worst.

By the time we got Shelly, MaryLayne was a fixture in our lives, a welcome visitor and dear friend, who would often stay for dinner if her timing was right. She had no set work schedule because she was too old to be employed by the state anyway. She worked past the retirement time, and stayed on for at least three years more, working long hours for no pay. She wanted to feel useful, and working helped stave off her deep depressions.

Eventually, I suppose, it became an unexplainable situation for the state, so they insisted she put her short-hand away and vacate the building as part of her retire-ment.

How did they do without her wealth of knowledge? She was surely missed by us, and though in many ways things became more organized, systematic and efficient, it never again had the special touch MaryLayne brought with her.

~ * ~

*"What is she doing?"*
*"I don't know."*
*"She looks like she's signing."*
*"No one is near her."*
*"She must be signing to the angels..."*

If you only know people when you are touching them, and hard rails of hospital beds surround you, your life is small. People who are in your room but out of your reach are out of your life, even if you are still in theirs.

The floor is only there for you when you are placed on it, the basket in the hall only exists for you if it is where you are at the moment.

So, when Shell left the hospital and came into our lives, we attempted to look at the world through her sight-less eyes, and define our company within the walls of her deafness.

In large part we didn't exist for her. She didn't hear us in the hall and call out to us. She didn't watch me fold her clothes across the room and clamor for my attentions. She never signed into the air—only into our hands. How could she conceive of us understanding without touch?

Soft things came into Shelly's life but most were quickly discarded. Teddy bears to the floor, blankets to the floor, dolls to the floor, and for many years—clothes to the floor, too. Shelly was tactilely defensive.

Our house is a zoo. Within our walls dogs, cats, birds, and assorted wildlife were always passing through.

Putting a kitten on Shelly's bed, or a dove in her hand, made me hope for the whole Annie Sullivan/Helen Keller moment. I wanted her to suddenly open up to a whole new world of tactile enjoyment, to grasp some elusive meaning about life and possibly make attempts to speak, sign frantically, or perform some other romantic daydreaming notion from my fantasies. Unfortunately, Shelly never saw the play or read the script.

Still, the dogs fascinated her and she fascinated them. Unlike the unlucky teddy bears, they moved on their own accord, and while it was hard for her to accept the soft fur, she deigned to pet them with my guidance. She laughed at them, she allowed them in her circle from time to time—she tolerated them.

For their part, the dogs sensed her helplessness, which is not the same as weakness. They were protective, and her erratic behaviors or movements did not worry them.

My cocker spaniel Emily lived with her own sight problems, having juvenile cataracts since puppy hood. She stayed clear of Shelly whenever possible even as she shadowed me constantly. Just as well, no one needed the blind leading the blind.

Overly protective of Shell, our white mutt, Max,

needed to be corralled into a separate room when company came. Max would have gone to any length to save Shelly if needed. As it was, he stayed firmly between his 'charge' and any visitors. I extend my apologies to any social workers, therapists, or birth parents who were terrorized by Max's zeal to guard the blind kid.

Charlie entered our lives as a two-year-old, handsome red Golden Retriever. There are treasures to be found at your local dog pound. All eighty-three pounds of blind Shelly tripped and fell on Charlie the first night he spent with us in his new home. He never flinched, never jumped up. He just gently looked at this child, understanding she meant him no harm, and let her fumble her way off him. I've trusted Charlie with her completely since then, and he's never let me down.

Then we got Belle, our 'caregiver' dog. Another Golden rescued dog, Belle came with strong nanny instincts. By then, Shelly was our only child at home but child-sized at eighteen, and Belle adopted her right away. She watched her, nuzzled around her, and became devoted to her. Reluctant at first, Shell soon started giggling at every encounter, encouraging Belle's attentions.

So Belle became Shell's dog. When Shell made her daily sweep of the recliner, intent on clearing it of objects and people, she often found Belle there, asleep. Instead of insisting the dog debark, she twirled the chair, around and around to both of their delight. They adored everything about each other.

Once, during a grave illness, Belle was all the more attentive, mooning around Shelly, sensing the seriousness of it all. Shell stayed asleep when a hospice nurse began taking her blood pressure, accustomed as she was to all these procedures.

As she woke, she slowly reached over to feel the nurse and identify her, but Belle put her front paws on the bed, and they were the first thing Shelly encountered. She followed them with her hand, up to the soft ears and long-muzzle. Shelly rose up on the bed to check again, obviously surprised Belle could take her blood pressure.

~ *Eight* ~

*We,* who have sight, use face recognition. Hearing/blind people often use voice recognition, but what of the deaf/blind? It's not very easy to know who you're dealing with when you're deaf/blind. There are various methods, such as identifying hands, rings or faces, but Shelly searched out earrings.

I suppose the reason earrings attracted Shell's attention was her daily exposure to female nurses. Not a bad method of discriminating one person from the other, I think. Shifts would change, aides would come and go, and doctors would be in and out, so she would feel and remember people from the earrings of that particular day, and I'm supposing, start all over the next day.

The nurses who were closest to Shell, her 'family nurses', would wear the same earrings every shift with her. Most of the time she would just explore the earrings, lightly touching, but occasionally she'd catch a finger in a hoop and end up pulling, doing some damage and taking out her temper on the nurse.

When it came to men, Shell's sensitive fingers would find the beard, even if recently shaved, and scarcely give the ears a touch, but I've seen her do a blind double-take when she came across a male nurse who wore an earring. She felt his jaw line, then his ear, and back to his jaw. When she confirmed to herself both the beard and the earring were there, she giggled helplessly.

I wore a pair of cheap stud earrings when I met Shelly and remembered to wear them when I went back to take her home from the hospital. Maybe I would have chosen others if I'd have known I'd be wearing the same pair for so many years to come. Whenever one of them wore out from her constant twisting and fiddling, I would send

Tom on an exacting, often frustrating search for the same kind.

Shelly used my earrings as a security blanket of sorts, hanging on while she fell asleep in my arms. I'd get tired of it eventually, but it's hard to break any habit in this child.

One day after taking my earrings out for a shower, I misplaced them. Like a toddler's pacifier, I decided Shelly really didn't need them, so I didn't search for long. Shell explored my ear at every contact with me and that night went to bed agitated. The next day as she headed for school, I was too busy to think about earrings, but later Shelly kept looking, pulling me down for a careful search.

Three days later I came across my studs and put them in. By then Shelly was acting very withdrawn, even while in my arms, so I assumed she was not feeling well. To cheer her up, I went in and 'showed' her my earrings. Her reaction tore at my heart, and I've never taken my place lightly in her life again. She cried. Shelly, who almost never cries - even when I know she is in great pain - cried. And she laughed at the same time. She hugged me sobbing and said "Amama", which is her only word, and rarely used. For a long time neither of us let go of the other, her hand clinging to my ear.

If you were a child and your mom came to you looking completely different, you could know from all the normal things she does, or her voice, or just because you, well- knew - it was your mom. But perhaps you'd start to doubt her if she continued to look like someone else.

Shell must have thought I had abandoned her.

Shell's lack of vision
Keeps my eyes on her
Always-

Claire Muller          Signing to the Angels

Her lack of hearing
Makes me listen to her
More.

~ *Nine* ~

*In* her preschool years, Michelle attended our nearby Early Childhood Development Center and an interesting issue came to light.

It was there that Shelly had her first real experience in dealing with many other children. In truth, this meant nothing to her. She didn't deal with them at all—so we needed to deal with her not dealing.

The teachers sent home reports of Shelly's bad behavior. I assumed she lashed out at others because she felt bad, maybe a stomach ache. Her skills at communicating her pain in a socially acceptable way were nil.

I had known the teachers from this wonderful place for years, and knew them to be people of patience—past most human boundaries. So when they said Shelly disrupted the class, they weren't just whining over some small matter.

In actuality, Shell had a complete disregard of anyone she didn't realize was there anyway. The teachers would hand her an object to explore and Shell would have no interest in holding it, so she would toss it over her shoulder, striking whoever happened to be behind her. She acted incapable of handing it back like a civilized little monkey.

The Center called in a respected psychologist who worked with children. He observed Shelly for a day and recognized the difficulty in addressing this behavior. From a sighted, hearing point of view, she was wrong. From a blind, deaf point of view, what's the big deal? Out of hand, out of mind.

So, the attempt was made to teach Shelly to hold a random object given to her, and hand it back to the giver when she was 'finished'. This galled my little redhead, who

40

felt it intruded on her personal space to respond in any genteel manner, and she refused to do it, getting angrier and craftier about throwing the object.

One suggestion by the doctor was an attempt to stop her temper tantrums long enough to retrieve the toy and get a moment to reward the good behavior. He suggested quick, well-timed cold water on her back may do the trick, though I believe he was cautious with his recommendation, as some may be offended by the approach.

I thought it sounded worth trying... after all, it's a splash of cold water, for heaven's sake – not like we were going to water-board her. It worked instantly and for a very short time. Then she went back to tossing things on principle.

So the Helen Keller Day happened.

I kept Shelly home from school, which was fine since they were thinking of making me do so anyway, I'm sure. I got her dressed in order to raise her expectations and make the day as normal as possible.

In the kitchen, I placed a little red rocking chair she loved to sit in, and got a variety of toys within reach, similar to what they were using at school.

I handed Shelly the first toy, a little matchbox car, and she promptly threw it over her shoulder. I took her by the hand and made her leave the rocker and feel around until she found the toy, and she got back into her seat, giggling. So much for the only levity she found for the next three hours. She threw it immediately, and we repeated the process. I knew if I could get her to hold it for even a moment, something longer than a second, I could praise her and we could move on. All the humor Shelly felt in the first few seconds of doing something different changed into irritation at not being allowed to do what she wanted, and then frustration, and then full-blown-knock-down-drag-out-anger.

Sensing an event of Olympic proportions, I planned

nothing else for the morning. I do admit that I believed it would likely take no more than half an hour or so. As I prepared for a challenge, I came with a huge store of patience that stayed with me during the whole ordeal.

And ordeal it certainly was. I wished afterwards I had a set up the camcorder. I was dressed in jeans, a sweatshirt over my t-shirt for the cold October day, but within an hour, I had stripped down to a tank top and bare feet.

When Shelly got angry she would first rip out her hearing aids, pull them completely apart and throw each piece far and wide. Then her shirt would go, and often her G-tube would be pulled out too. On this day, it took everything I could muster to keep any clothes on her at all, finally being satisfied to retain the pull-up.

Shelly didn't want to pick up the stupid toy. As soon as her bottom hit the rocker's seat, the offending car went flying. Over and over, time after time, we played it out. Angry enough to be grunting and shrieking, hitting and biting, she hurled herself against me, against anything she could find, using the rocker as a weapon when she could.

Both of us were growing more and more exhausted, and I began to think this was hopeless. I pictured the struggle going through the night, and both of us falling to the floor in a heap, unable to ever move again. We slid on the floor, slippery with our sweat, and the bruises on me were partly from being attacked, and partly from protecting Shelly against self-inflicted wounds as she cast herself into counters, flailing her arms against cabinets, throwing herself to the floor.

The more she fought, the more a calm patience wrapped around me like a blanket. I was determined to "win" but was thrilled and awed at the force I was up against in this little child. She was marvelous in her anger - a Hellion, a wildcat, a savage wonder. She was a Helen Keller! I didn't want her any different, and part of me grieved that what I was so determined to get from her, needed to get from her to make her acceptable around others - would also change her. I didn't want to break her spirit, but I would have to tame it.

The end came abruptly, after three hard-fought hours. I had just physically manipulated Shelly's whole body, like a controlling shadow covering her, arm over arm, hand over hand, making her pick up the little car against every fiber of her will, and making her sit again in the red rocker. That very moment Tom, coming home, opened the door wide and a blast of frigid air hit the half-naked, sweating child, and she froze in place, unmoving, the toy in hand. It was all I had asked of her, and I took what I could get, involuntary or not, hugging her and applauding her, "good job!"

She surrendered.

I took the toy from her in the socially acceptable manner, then handed it back. She held it and cried for a moment, breaking my tired heart in two. Then, by the sweetness of mercy, she started rolling the car up and down her own belly, finding out how to play with it—my turn to cry.

## ~ *Ten* ~

I'm forever changed knowing...
Shell's life on this earth has been
More for us than for her.

All who are linked with this child
Are blessed from her small, quiet world.
She was never here to learn,
But to teach.

This is how it is with some children-
Not 'what might have been'
But what is.

And the truth is-
They couldn't possibly be more perfect.
I question if we're worthy of this lesson,
Given by a life -
It has humbled my heart.

When we know what depth,
What sorrow,
What hell, what joy, what pain,
What loss,

What sweetness we hold,
And can't possibly deserve...
We are changed.


Whitney McNiel is young, but she is brave. She
learns the ropes: how to hook and unhook, what medicines
and how much, what responses to make. She doesn't dwell

on 'what-if's'. What if she forgets something? What if she makes a mistake? What if Shell wants something and can't tell her what it is?

What if, what if, what if?

Because Whitney is brave, we have some respite, occasional outings with the other kids, meetings and trainings, the occasional distant family events.

Bravery is hard to come by.


"Apparently, Shell has something called 'Hemolytic-Uremic Syndrome'," I said to Tom in a phone call from a local hospital. I had rushed her there when she showed symptoms we had never encountered, bleeding from everywhere, it seemed.

The day only got more horrible as the staff became fixated on all Shelly's 'normal' problems, like a non-working gut, dependency on IV's, blind-deafness. Precious time was being wasted - explaining over and over what was conventional for this unconventional child, apart from this unexpected illness. Granted, Shell comes with a lot of baggage, but as they kept trying to fix what she always had I watched her change for the worse by the moment.

In addition to this confusion, the hospital had no pediatric-gastroenterologist on staff, and we didn't happen to show up on the day the visiting one was expected. After two days I gave up. Against the hospital's best advice, but supported by our doctor in Columbus, I withdrew her, and headed her to the airport to catch a flight.

Michelle felt rotten, still bleeding from random places. Even if she didn't know about it, it was upsetting to me. As we headed up the ramp for the plane, I realized there'd been a delay somewhere ahead with many people yet in line to board.

I usually held her in the waiting area until I knew we could get on smoothly. No turning back now, so I twirled her, bounced her, and prayed we'd get through this flight.

Living through seemingly endless, difficult moments like this, I envision myself tucked into bed at night, the drama behind me, almost as if I could will the time to fast-forward.

Finally, getting in the door to the plane, there was another delay from a passenger with a stuck overhead bag. Screaming her anger at this point, Shell thrashed around, pulling at everything in reach of her grasping hands. I ducked with her into the space used by the flight attendants for fixing coffee.

If I could have, I would have gotten back off. I felt completely out of options and sense, second guessing my decision to take her from the hospital. We finally got to our seat and she settled down somewhat, though still kicking the seat ahead of her from time to time, and making her alien noises. The man in front of us turned and asked if I could 'please control her!' I was mortified, without words to respond to his harshness as I tried to distract my hurting, angry child.

I was paying the other passengers little attention, being mentally, visually and physically focused on Shelly, so I was surprised to find a tap on my arm coming from a woman with a friendly face. I had been half-expecting a flight attendant bouncer to hand me a written injunction against flying with this tempestuous child ever again on this airline.

"I noticed your little girl. What beautiful hair! Would it be all right if I gave her this? I bought it to give to a niece for Christmas, but I'd love to give it to your daughter instead," the woman said in a soft voice.

She held out a small white bag. Flustered with her kindness, I only stammered some form of a 'thank you' as she went back to her seat in the rear of the plane.

During a relatively quiet moment from Shell, I opened the lightweight bag to find a paper mache ornament of a clown, smiling from a prone position. Exquisitely done, bright and cheerful, it was given with such under-standing and compassion.  My heavy heart lightened immeasurably. What a Godsend to me and my hurting, in-nocent child.

I glimpsed the woman one last time in the airport, giving us a small wave and as Shelly hangs that ornament on our tree every year, the woman's kindness to a harried stranger comes back to me each Christmas.

Angels surround us.

## ~ *Eleven* ~

*S*helly acted just the slightest bit different the other day - a signal to me to pay more attention, to check for fever, listen to her lungs or watch her gait while she's walking.

It got me thinking of what it's like to care for her. It's as if I'm at the top of a high cliff and Shelly is dangling over the straight long fall, holding onto my hand. Much of the time, things are fine, I'm strong and my grip on her is good.

Then there are days I feel her slipping and I hold on tighter. I reposition myself to take better care, my heart beats faster in fear for her, and my adrenalin kicks in. I sleep lighter, listening. I stand and watch her breathing.

I've gotten hints in the past from people who don't know us very well, suggesting she'd be better off if I let her go. I don't know or care if she'd "be better off". Perhaps all of us would - perhaps fewer than you'd suppose.

But it doesn't matter to me. I could no more let go on purpose than I could walk myself into a lake and keep going until I drowned. Life is stronger than we think, and I'm instinctively tightening myself around her when she needs me most, protecting her life, for better or worse. I simply can do no less.

It astounds me sometimes just how strange life is. A healthy child will fall from a ladder on the playground and die on a sunny afternoon. A moment here and the next he's gone. A baby will sleep in a wrong position and never wake up again. A stumble, the flu, a car running a red-light...

But here is my girl - brushing by death so closely I can feel the breath from it - and she lives.

She lives past her 10th birthday, a morning I woke to see her so far gone. "So, you were to be here ten years exactly, my Bean?" I whispered. She lives past acute and massive septic infections in her hip, high fevers from septic lines, pneumonia in both lungs, and a gut with no rhyme or reason.

She lives through and past surgeries whose long scars sear across her stomach. She survives lines burrowed into her jugular and sub-clavian veins. She lives.

And she lives without all the external cues we get as sighted and hearing people, confirming life is to be fought for—a beautiful sunset, the sound of her Papa reading her a book.

She lives without all the promises of a future, keeping so many of us going—a walk down the aisle, college and career, children of our own.

She lives and reminds me daily—God is good.

## ~ Twelve ~

*When* Julie came into our lives...

Julie's last day to work with Shelly is more memorable to me than her first. On her first day I didn't know what the future held or what doors would be opened to our child by this confident, very young, home schooled girl whose main recommendation for the new position was her signing ability and vision for Shell's future.

I didn't know she would be the first of several intervenors, because at the time we hired her, we didn't even know what an 'intervenor' was or did. (I later likened it to Annie Sullivan's relationship with Helen Keller).

I didn't know the self-assured enthusiasm Julie began with would continue and she would be Shell's advocate in the school system as well as her eyes and ears, friend and teacher.

The sun scorched a cloudless sky on her last working day. Julie and Michelle were back from the state park pool where, as usual, they were admitted for free. With the exuberance Julie showed in teaching Shelly, she naturally involved everyone around her in the process, making people want to help. She invited the questions of small children, who even at toddler ages seemed to know immediately that there was something different about this alien child.

The lifeguards at the pool let them use the slide during their breaks, not minding the extra duty to watch them. Shell loved the water with a passion and fearlessness, not knowing depths and heights. It was a perfect chance to learn many signs not otherwise used, and nothing made her happier than to feel the signs, 'You-go-swimming!'

I dreaded this last day. Part of me kept hoping when

it came down to it, Julie would change her mind. I found it hard to believe she could leave us, go off and get a real life with a husband and children... Surely she'd forsake everything, or at least put it off – forever!

But she *was* leaving, just as Annie Sullivan moved on and left Helen. I finally and reluctantly accepted the loss.

The remainder of the afternoon was spent in riotous play in the back yard. Julie filled a big cooler with packing peanuts and water for Shell to climb into. Another cooler filled with water balloons ended up exploding on everyone and everything. Shell was in high spirits, giggling at every new sensation. My other kids joined the fun - one of the perfect, happy days of Shelly's world.

I knew Julie would always be in our lives, but watching her say goodbye to Shell was heartbreaking. She always brought passion, and a sense of fun along with the words and experiences, and we would miss her greatly.

Of course, she would never trade the path she took, the choice of her life with Josh and having eleven amazing children, but I suspect she is one of those people who wished they could have lived two lives.

*~ Julie Lanier Witt, Intervenor ~*
*"Write a bit on what Shelly meant to your life."*
*Claire said.*

*Wow, how does one begin such a tale? I recall the many times Shelly taught the teacher. I don't remember all of the things she couldn't do, but how she did what she did with what she had.*

*I will never forget the first time I saw Shelly. About five years old, she came with Claire's family to one of the home school achievement nights our small group put on every year. As a thirteen year old I was fascinated at the way she maneuvered fearlessly around the stage and explored everything she could get her hands on. "How could she be so brave when the world is so big and she is so small and disadvantaged by her handicaps?" I wondered.*

*Shelly had two things many perfectly "whole" people never have: A mom with the fiercest loyalty and devotion I have ever witnessed and an unquenchable spirit.*

*My entire time in high school and beginning college, I often thought of Shelly and wondered how she was doing. I saw her on several occasions and my interest in her fed my desire to pursue special/deaf education as a career.*

*After my second year in the deaf-ed program at EKU, Claire approached me about becoming Shelly's intervener. I was immediately excited about the idea, but was I equipped for the job? We decided I would begin working with her part time and see how it went. 'How do I start with this little person who had no formal language to use?' I wondered, unsure of myself.*

*Soon I realized the key: gain her trust and find things she wanted from me.*

*At first it was a challenge. She did not appreciate me making her work for the things she wanted. I remember going home with scratches on my hands and totally worn out that first week. But the initial hurdle was crossed - she realized I was not backing down. She soon proved she could do the signs I wanted from her and we were off like a rocket.*

*As soon as Shelly's love of any kind of physical movement became clear to me, I used it to every advantage possible. Unlike Anne Sullivan with Helen Keller, Shelly was not motivated by food, so finding things she wanted badly enough to work for proved challenging. Movement was the key. She must learn to make the connection of the sign with the action, and Shelly loved action.*

*In a matter of days she learned the signs for ride, swing, jump, play, spin, and more. After learning the initial sign, it was nothing for her to begin adding my name and other words to the action to make complete senten-*

ces. I could not believe how quickly she picked up on everything - everything she considered meaningful.

Claire started talking to me about Perkins Institute
for the Blind in Boston and how they had a summer ap-
prenticeship program accepting applications. I immediately
started looking into their deaf/blind school and became
extremely excited. I interviewed for one of their spots,
was accepted, and went to work there for three months. I
will never forget that eye-opening experience. I learned so
much both in the classrooms and in the life experience lessons with the students there. Every day, I would think
about how to relate all of the things learned there, to my
work with Shelly in the upcoming school year. I could not
wait to get back and see her.

Kentucky did not have a large population of high
functioning deaf/blind children, so I felt lost many times
with no real curriculum to follow or experienced people to
help me. Following Shelly's lead and Claire's instincts
seemed the best path to follow.

Our routine each day included me going to her
house, walking her through the steps of bathing and dressing herself and getting ready for the school day. It was
such a joy to see her become more independent each day
and watch her calm down and anticipate the next step in
the routine. As with many children with handicaps, the
routine of the day became her anchor to identify with and
gave her a sense of security.  We would then drive to
school and begin a day of more structured learning.

Not having a lot of hands-on objects to use for her, I
ended up making quite a few texture book and other items
we could use in the school. We would both grow very frustrated at times when the required participation in
"school" activities became an exercise in un-meaningful
waiting and boredom for this child who could not see or
hear any of the events.

By far, our favorite type of learning involved 'get in

53

and get dirty' sort of things. We loved the days we could go swimming, play in the dirt, make things with shaving cream, and more. Each opportunity gave us many occasions to try out new words and experience new things.

As I look over the journal I kept during our time together, it is amazing to see how she began with about four signs. When those were mastered, the list grew to over 100 in a little over 5 months. What a smart little lady! It amazed me to see her go from doing only what I required of her to get what she wanted, to watching her take the initiative and start conversations or ask for something unprompted.

An excerpt from my journal:

10/18/94: "She did the neatest thing today! While riding in the car, she reached over for my arm and found my hand. This is unusual because she rarely touches me in the car. She pulled on my hand with both of hers as far as it would go. Then, she tapped on the window and tried to sign 'down'. Amazing feat without a prompt."

Even after such a short time working together, the turning point of initiating conversations and requests had begun.

Shelly was so beautiful. I remember watching her concentrate intently on an activity with her little head bent down, her silky red hair falling on her smooth white cheeks and wondering why she had been dealt this hand in life. She challenged my faith daily as I saw someone so visibly at a disadvantage to most people, get up each day with a fierce desire to learn and grow. She did not dwell on the things she was missing - only what was out there for her to do next.

I remember when we would be working on a new sequence of signs and she would know what the end result would be when she got it right. She would bounce up and down with excitement while she trying to perfect the signs and flash a huge grin when I placed her hand on my cheek *and nodded, letting her know she had gotten it right. We would then swing, or bounce or move and she would laugh with delight. How I wish all people could have experienced this pure joy.*

*I could say much more, but will stop now. Let me end with stating clearly how blessed I was to have Shelly as part of my life. The ways I learned from her and grew as a result of her presence in my life can never be expressed fully. I miss you, little lady.*

## ~ *Thirteen* ~

*Sh*ell and I had been up at Columbus Childrens' for a week, but I needed to leave her there and go home to my other young children. A few days later the doctor called to release her, so I scrambled to make plans to get to the hospital. Tom was on duty at the fire department, and I was stuck without a vehicle. When I called to update our pediatrician's office, I spoke with our friend and Dr.Ron's nurse, Nancy. She insisted that her husband Butch would be happy to drive me to the airport.

When Butch offered help he meant it. He looked you in the eye when he asked how things were going and listened to the answer. His quiet gentle spirit lifted the mood of those around him. This day he was a God-send.

We left the house an hour before my seven o'clock flight. Things were more relaxed in those days at airports. Traffic jammed the front of the terminal and though Butch offered to come in, I assured him I'd be fine. He dropped me off at the entrance and I waved, assuming everything would go smoothly, traveling childless.

Inside, I was surprised to see a large throng swarming the counter. I stood clueless on the outskirts, not sure where the actual line began. Finally something a man said penetrated my reverie and I looked at the boards to see my flight in the process of being canceled. I recalled Butch had been driving through a heavy fog, but apparently the fog in my mind was even thicker, as it never occurred to me we'd be prevented from flying. Stranded in this age before common cell phones, Butch was long gone.

I wandered near a group of businessmen, likewise marooned; one of them noticed me and asked if I would like to join them. They were going to rent a vehicle and get as far as Cincinnati to catch other flights. I was grateful for having risen early enough for a shower, and with a skirt and some make-up, I looked half-way presentable. There is no way I would have been invited along in my normal attire of jeans and old coat, Shelly in tow.

It was not the first time I suspected some of Shell's angels also guarded me. Trusting soul that I am, I acepted, and the men went off to secure a car. I stepped outside to my very first limo ride!

There were five men; two sat next to me facing the other three in the spacious interior, glassed off from the driver. I looked like the novice I was, but I think they all enjoyed seeing someone get this kind of rare treat.

Leaving the airport grounds, the men took turns introducing themselves, telling me their various lines of work. A strong accent made me concentrate on one of them and I couldn't resist asking about it. He came from Poland, and I pressed him for details of how he came to be an American. He hesitated at first, but since it's easier at times to speak openly with strangers, he told us his story of being a boy of eight when World War II broke out and Germans overran his village in Poland.

He and his older brother left their parents and sisters to flee the country, traveling only at night, being shot at once as they crossed a barbed wire border. The boys never saw their family again, lost to the war, and neither brother ever returned to Poland, even all these years later. Miles and time flew by too quickly, listening to his fascinating story.

Arriving at the Cincinnati airport, the men brushed off my attempts to help pay for the car. They assured me it was a tax write-off, but sharing it with me was still a treasured gift and a kindness.

After another long hospitalization I again returned alone to Shelly, flying on an exceptionally hot day. We passed through some rough weather, causing the plane to dip and shake erratically. I sat next to a girl in her early twenties dressed in a heavy plaid overcoat, scarf loosely hung around her sweaty neck. She kept her head down, long brown hair disheveled and eyes shut for most of the flight. Make-up couldn't hide shades of green on her face and she white-knuckled the arm rests, obviously near tears. I tried to distract her, telling her about Shell's joy in rough weather flying, her joy in turbulence. It made me love turbulence, too.

Sheepishly, the girl admitted to wearing the same clothes on this flight as she had on the only other flight she had taken.

"Let me guess." I said. "Freezing cold winter day that time?"

"Well the plane didn't crash, so they're lucky! I'm not flying without them." She laughed at herself, overdressed in wool on such a steamy day, and relaxed enough to chat for the rest of the flight. Our flights were delayed in Cincinnati, so we ate lunch, took pictures and parted. I've thought of her often since then, praying she flies safe.

## ~ *Fourteen* ~

### ~ Nancy Donta, Deaf/Ed Teacher ~

*I* was Shelly's teacher, at least in the official relationship. Actually, over the years, I feel sure she taught me far more than I ever taught her. I still think about and use the lessons she so diligently taught me in both my professional and personal life.

I taught hearing impaired students in another district when I got a call from Clark County schools.

"Would I be interested in working with a homebound student with deaf-blindness?"

I always loved a good challenge in my career and told them I would try anything once. When I first met Shelly, she had just been released from the hospital, yet again, and we were to start homebound instruction. At eight years old, she looked so small and pale - almost translucent skin - with breathtaking, long flaming-red hair. Claire patiently explained her condition, rocking as she spoke. Shelly wore only a pull-up and a huge bandage over her heart.

What have I gotten myself into? *I wondered, as I talked about my ideas to teach her.*

Fortunately, God prepared me to be Shelly's teacher without me realizing it. Over the previous years He had sent me many students with bits of information I then applied to her. She taught me the rest.

I had been told she was medically fragile - and she was. I knew someday she would be back in the hospital bed permanently. While she was healthy, I wanted to "make memories" so she would have good times to think about always. I was blessed I got the very best of Shelly. We did make memories.

Afraid of nothing, she skirts a room -
A waiting room, an office, a classroom, a church.

Her fingers go from one object to another,
Details explored,
Care taken.
A curious monkey - not a blundering bull.

Does she move bravely toward stairs –
Or blindly?
Both, I think. With no hesitation
She takes them up...
She takes them down.

Finding a person she touches ears and face - feels
jewelry.
Prompted, she signs 'Hi' - hugs and waves 'Goodbye'

But she means, 'Time for you to move.'

She may trip on something,
Fall, and laugh at herself.
She must be guarded from sharp or hot - treacher-
ous traps as she makes her way-
Feeling everything.

In time, she finds me again...
"Did you glance around the place?" I asked.

*I hope she's sturdier than she looks*, I thought, upon finally meeting Becca. We had been talking on and off for more than a year before coming face to face.

Becca attended Cincinnati Christian University when she heard we were lookin for an intervenor. She called, hoping we may possibly consider her for the position in a year when she graduated. Even from a young age, watching the Helen Keller Story, she wished for the chance to work with a deaf/blind child. There are not very many opportunities.

I'd almost forgotten about her initial contact when I got her second call. A year is a long time, plenty of time to change one's mind about their future, especially when they are heading out in the world of possibilities.

After many phone calls and a growing hope on my part, we finally met in person. In appearance, Becca was just a slip of a girl, cheerful and lively. I hoped she could hold her own with Michelle.

And hold her own she did. Almost as soon as we hired her, we asked her to join us for a trip to Anaheim, California, to attend the deaf/blind part of the National Federation of the Blind Conference. While there, we all got to learn and interact with other deaf/blind and Becca had a lot of hands-on time with Shell, but without all the responsibility. She had the chance to watch us as a family, and we could see if she was made of sturdy enough stuff to take on the Bean.

They clicked. And for much of the next seven years Becca was part of our Shelly family.

*~ Becca Morrow, Intervenor ~*
*The summer after I graduated from college, I started working with Shelly. At ten years old, she barely looked six. Her hair was red and she had the temper reputed to go with it. I would be her intervener or one-on-one assistant. When I would talk to her, Shelly would hold my hands and I would sign words. When she signed to me, she felt I should hold her hands. She could be quite insistent.*

*I have a lifetime of memories from my time with Shelly. Sometimes I'm not sure who learned more. I may Have taught her 'things,' but she taught me to appreciate life. I got to experience so much with this wonderful girl.*

*Life will sometimes trigger a particular moment with her. I see her face tilted up to the sky, smile on her face, angelic giggle on the air.*

*One of my favorite memories with Shelly was a trip to the local K-Mart to look for a hat. We ended up sitting on the floor with a pile and I would hand them to her one at a time. She would put them on and either take them off immediately or turn them around on her head. If she threw them off immediately, we put them in the "no" pile. If she took more time with them, we put them in a "maybe" pile.*

*I then handed her the hats from the "maybe" pile again, one at a time. This time she felt them in more detail until she ended up with the perfect one. The final choice was a big red hat, the brim folded up in the front with a big flower attached. Together we put all the other hats back where we found them. She helped me pay for the hat and walked out wearing it, smiling her way to the car. The tag stayed with the hat and I'd call her Minnie Pearl whenever she wore it.*

*My job started as a summer position. As it got closer to the school year, I interviewed with the school system and became Shelly's school intervener.*

*Arriving at school she'd hang up her jacket and backpack, and then start her morning by checking her calendar box. This was a series of cubbies, holding representations, or object cues, for her day. For example, the object cue for the playground was mulch, because mulch covered the playground. Shelly delivered newspapers to the classrooms, so the object cue was newspaper. Whenever Shell finished with one activity she put the object cue in her 'finished bucket'. At the end of the day she would have to go through the 'finished bucket' and talk about each item. She picked three object cues to put in her journal for that day.*

*When I took her home, she would find her mom and*

*then come to me. She would take my hands and make me say, "Bye-bye, Shelly". And she would say, "Bye-bye, Becca," and wave to me. She didn't want to find me there after she said good-bye. If she did find me there after we said good-bye, she would be a little more expressive in her gestures. Later, if she found I stayed on to talk - still there - she would move me closer to the door forcibly signing 'good-bye'.*

*My time with Shelly was some of the most wonderful and challenging of my life. I always knew I wanted to work with the deaf in some way. Shelly resulted in a richer dream than the one I had for myself. Isn't it nice when dreams not only come true, but explode to more than you could have imagined? Shelly was not just a job for me. She was a fulfillment of my dream, my companion, my life. She will always be my friend, my Shelly.*

~ * ~

Saying Michelle could throw a fit is an understatement.

She might wake up in the night angry, perhaps not feeling well, mostly dealing with horrible gas, unable to tell anyone where and what hurt. She would slam about, crashing into the sides of the bed, hurling objects, and emitting a high pitched yell-scream combination.

It would make me rise straight up from the bed like a mummy from a fright flick and leap to her side, hoping to prevent damage. Sometimes I was too late and she would have pulled out her G-tube, or worse yet, pulled apart her Broviac line. After several frustrating trips for repairs at a local hospital, I learned how to fix them myself. It involves glue, is kind of crafty and therefore is just up my alley. We needed to keep a fresh kit on hand at all times and sometimes she would use two in a week.

Some of her conniption fits would take place when Shell was up and ready for schoo, or even at school. For those, she usually started with a sudden attack of the hear-

63

Ing aid, and before anyone could react, would have the aid pulled from her ear, dismantled into small pieces, and thrown in every direction possible.

While we scurried around to find the precious missing parts before a dog could eat them, or another child could - well... eat them - Shell would start ripping off her clothes. By ripping, I mean literally ripping; the arms of her shirts, any buttons in reach, hats and belts. Then off came the shoes and socks, thrown with amazing accuracy for a blind child at anyone within reach.

Ah, that child could throw a fit.

Laguna Beach
Shell's first feel of waves—touching
Her toes,
Indescribable delight in the coming
And the going
The give of sand under her feet,
Her arms around my legs as the waves crash
Into us
Squealing in joy at the breadth of it all.

Even blind she was aware -
The enormity...
Even deaf she felt the vibration -
The ocean waves...
She was enthralled
And we were there to see it -

The best day.
Shelly's best day ever.

~ *Fifteen* ~

*"What matters deafness of the ears when the mind hears? The true deafness, the incurable deafness, is that of the mind." (Victor Hugo)*

We made arrangements with Perkins School for the Blind in Boston, for Shell to be evaluated there.

She had been in school for three years by then and her daily joy from the first year replaced in the second year by being 'mostly willing'. The third year, marked by tantrums and anger made me question what was going on in class. Most of her daily reports came in the form of how many tantrums she threw, or if she cooperated. I often railed at the activities, seemingly designed to bore or confuse her, so I found myself on a very different page, too often, with her schooling. I wanted to get a fresh perspective, from people who daily dealt with deaf-blind children, to determine if Shell was 'teachable', or merely trainable.

Perkins stunned me. *What* a place. Chris Underwood, who had been back and forth with me on the phone, had us meet with several evaluators who impressed me instantly with their ability "see" my child. They took her through a day of both physical and mental gymnastics, concluding Shell was just as bright and intelligent as I thought. I daydreamed of a Shelly with a working gut, blindness and deafness as her 'only' problems. I would have found a way for her to go there every day.

*"I will not leave you."*
*"I will look as if I were suffering. I would look a little as if I were dying. It is like that. Do not come to see that. It is not worth the trouble."*
*"I shall not leave you." (Le Petit Prince)*

How can fear can be felt physically spreading through your body? Starting somewhere low and creeping through your limbs, into your mind, until you feel there is some sort of spell over your hands as they go about their work. How is it possible to see what you are doing, as if looking at someone else doing it? How can your adrenaline stay so high, normal motions seeming like slow motion?

I held Shelly on the ball last night. She appeared to be fine when I got her up, and I'm nothing if not observant of her. We bounced there as usual for almost an hour, when she gave a different breath.

Just like that she went from normal to scaring me. It was slight, and may have escaped the attention of someone who was not her mama, but very soon it became more obvious, every breath congested. She sounded then like someone who'd been nursing a cold for several days, instead of several minutes.

Her nose started to run and by the time I sat with her in our recliner, I felt her temperature change, also. Her hands grew cold; only her back felt hot, but I know her too well, and put the thermometer under her arm. Her normal temp is 96.7 and she was up to 99.8 by then. Soon after I got her in bed, snuggled in the soft warm nightgown Tom just bought for her, covered lightly in her favorite blanket, cushioned on the softest pillow I could find, she began an occasional cough.

I went to bed, knowing I may be up with her often, but I was afraid and my sleep was a long time in coming. Suddenly, at five o'clock the next morning, Shell was obviously worse. Our store of medicines didn't include liquid Tylenol at the moment, so I gave her a dose of Nyquil. She fought off the drowsy effects with her usual determination, but was soon resting more comfortably.

I lay down again, fear overwhelming me. I don't know a better word than dread. I dread her hurting; I dread her being unable to tell me how to help.

I have many selfish fears too. I am Shelly's mama. If I'm not Shelly's mama, then who am I? If someone else shared a similar story, I'd tell them they were still their own selves, of course, and another person can't define who you are, but it still doesn't feel true when I tell myself the same.

I'm Shelly's mama, her defender, her nurse, her friend, her line of communication. I'm the one who knows every speck of her—fingers, eyes, and scars. I'm the one who knows what she wants with every tiny nuance. How can I not be Shelly's mama anymore?

I dread the possibility of losing her. I just can't picture my life without her. I can't imagine not taking care of her, of her not being there to physically touch. I can't bear to think of not seeing her sweet face again.

So - selfishly I'm afraid. I'm afraid of her being gone and the hole of grief, of never filling in the lost places. I'm afraid of having to heal and go out and be normal. I'm afraid of facing people again, of going into stores, of making mistakes. I'm afraid of what I may find out about myself.

What if I can't relate to those out there anymore, the ones who have all the years I lack, of practice in social settings? What if I find I can't do it? What if I'm too overwhelmed by it all, and yet have to exist anyway? What if I disappoint Tom by not being able to do things, when I don't have Shelly as an excuse to be so isolated? What if all the things I think I'd like to do just slip away and I am lost?

Today she seems better, more like she's just fighting a cold. Likely she'll be fine, and this will just be one more weakening area. But the fear comes fast with every change, and I have all the questions unanswered every time she fades. I want to be with her for every moment, letting her feel how much I love her and so... keeping her from leaving me for good.

## ~ Sixteen ~

$\mathscr{I}$took Shell to the eye doctor one day...
So paperwork could be satisfied -
So questions could be satisfied -
So more paperwork could be satisfied -
I was sure she was blind...
She was...
Blind, that is...

The kind doctor looked deep into her eyes
With a little light resembling a pen -
She asked if Shelly ever poked her eyes... "No." I
said.
(She had never poked her eyes)
"Hum-m-m. That's good." The doctor said.

On the ride home from the doctor,
As if she'd heard,
As if her hearing worked,
As if she heard more than she saw...
Shell buried her thumbs deep into her eye sockets...
For good.

*~ Kim Pitts, Intervenor ~*
*One of my favorite memories of Shelly would be of
driving her home from school one day. Spring brought
warmth and we could actually roll down the windows. Shelly loved having the wind blow on her as we
drove down the road. She would hold her cupped hand just
a tad bit out of the window to where she would feel the
resistance of the wind pushing against it. I'll never forget
that laugh! After going down the road a ways, I caught on
to the pattern of Shelly's burst of laughter. Every time we*

would stop at a light for a second, she would sit there qui-etly, putting her hands behind her head, and then bust out in giggles as we started back on our way. I thought she was just feeling really good that particular day, enjoying the first warmth of spring.

Once we pulled up to her house, I got out and went around to help Shelly out of the car. I already knew she had kicked her shoes off. (Not uncommon at all for Shelly.... those darn clothes, she didn't know why we had to wear them anyway!) I opened the door and she just sat there with this huge smile on her face. I couldn't help but laugh. (Yeah... I was still clueless and she knew it.)

I looked in the floorboard for her shoes and they were nowhere to be found. I looked in between the seats and all through the back seat... still... shoes were nowhere to be found. Knowing she had them when she got in the car, I stood there talking to Shelly as if she could hear every word I said. "Shelly, what on earth have you done with your shoes?!?!"

And that's when I noticed the empty console. "Shelly! Where's my hairbrush? My house keys? My check-book?" And, as if Shelly heard every word I had just said, she began cackling and flailing her arms like I've never seen her do before. She cracked up!

At all those stoplights little Miss Innocent Shelly got so tickled about, she had thrown at least one item, if not two, out the window. I had to retrace my route back to the school as fast as I could. Aside from my embarrass-ment, jumping out and crossing the intersection at every light, I couldn't help but laugh the whole time! Miracu-lously, I retrieved all the important items. There's no telling how many she actually threw away.

It was just one of the many adventures Shelly took me on while working with her that year!! She's definitely someone who etched her name on my heart for eter-nity. Love you Bean!!!

69

## ~ Seventeen ~

*H*ave I mentioned this child is a redhead? Michelle is a redhead in every possible way - in every cliché and rumor.

Her temper is the first sign. If you were blind yourself, you'd know this child had red hair. She improved after anti-depressants, but if a thing is not her way - it is no way at all. Battle after lost battle shows me where my efforts stand in this war. I'm a loser.

Sometimes it's funny. Other times it's downright aggravating and once in a while it's even dangerous.

On the humorous side, I've seen others contest wills with Michelle and have enjoyed watching them change their minds about what seemed important before they presented it to her.

Those nurses who have cared for Shelly over the years know better, but when a new nurse makes the mistake of insisting Shell keep on a hospital wristband, it's best just to sit back and watch them become educated. Shell won't give up and can't hear the reason she'd not have listened to anyway. I've never, ever seen her lose a wristband struggle.

I'm sure hospital bands are important, but no one will convince Shell. The moment they go on she works them off. So the uninitiated nurse will try again, perhaps with less 'give' to the looseness and when it also goes flying, she tries the ankle. This is child's play to The Bean, and the nurse won't have her back turned before she finds herself stepping on it again.

I usually get 'the lecture' at this point, of the hospital safety concerns and issues and regulations and I can see her regular nurses snickering in the background. I've heard offers of taping the band to her back and other suggestions but it always comes down to the nurse finally suggesting, as if she was the first to think of it, that we can just tape it to her bed.

Again, if it's within finger reach, it's back on the floor, so it gets taped to the backside of the bed, where it finally gets to stay. I know it seems like a small thing, but Shelly is more stubborn than the rest of us and will have her way in the end.

It's more annoying to find myself unable to break bad habits, like eye poking or teeth grinding. I tap on her fingers or her lips for each of these aggravations, but she starts up again within moments, and I can't do squat about it.

When Shelly's hardheadedness became dangerous for her, we had to go to great lengths to correct the behavior. At one point Shell started destroying her IV lines on a regular basis. We were going in and out of Children's Hospital as if through a revolving door. Every line pulled out required surgery to replace, and every line torn apart meant difficult repairs and the strong possibility of septic infections.

At my wits end, I tried everything I could think of to stop her destructive behavior. I stood over her bed night after night to prevent her from tearing into this lifeline, but I was exhausted and still inefficient. Eventually you have to leave her for a trip to the bathroom or a little sleep.

Shelly knew this was an instant attention grabber, and I rewarded the behavior by being there constantly, but my choices were not happy ones. You can ignore a child who's holding their breath for attention, because they'll eventually want to breathe again. Shelly lived without parameters and felt free to wreak as much havoc as possible.

Obviously, her doctors knew about this and they had many conferences on the 'Shelly issue', I'm sure. Finally, they referred us to a Child Behavioral Psychologist on staff there at Children's and we spent much time discussing what could be done. He finally suggested a controversial treatment, rarely used, and then only in life-threatening situations such as this.

A few days later we found ourselves back in the hospital for yet another line repair and we all agreed it was necessary to give the treatment a try.

The doctor came in carrying a device developed by himself and another doctor. I inspected the little black box with a round, flat metal spot in the center of one side. He showed me how it would be placed on her leg, wrapped in an ace bandage with the smooth metal piece the size of a dime, close to her skin.

A second device would be hand-held by the observer, with a button to press and fire a shot of agonizing, excruciating, near lethal dose of horrendous pain charging through her arching body, long red hair erect, nails digging into palms, eyeballs rolling back in her head, obviously soon to be followed by cosmic seizure activity.

Oh, sorry. Just my own private fear of electricity coming out.

In truth, it felt like a quick tug on my arm hair. Nothing more and I know, because even though I really do fear electrical shocks, I strapped it to my arm and tried it out. I would never have agreed to it otherwise, and neither would her gentle doctor.

In fact, there was an overeager intern in the room at the time aspiring to be the first one to administer the 'charge' to Shell. The doctor told him to roll up his sleeve to feel it himself. When he chickened out, the doctor made him leave the room completely.

So, for a short while I dealt with Shelly's dangerous behavior without getting close to her. I say for a short while because she soon learned every way possible to take the box off, no matter its location, and also because she stopped pulling her IV line apart. I think she just decided it wasn't worth the fuss and began to be quite solicitous of her line, whenever possible keeping it from getting tangled or caught on anything.

I'm really grateful for this oddball therapy. Every line replacement, every line repair, every time Shelly messed with her Broviac, she risked sepsis and complications of surgeries, and death. Sometimes you just have to pick your poison, draw a line in the sand and commit to tough-love.

"Tonight is a Date-Night," I tell Tom.
(The boys were away for the night camping with
friends, and Shonta had gone to bed early.)
"A Date-Night?" he says, doubtfully.
"Yes", I say. "You with a cute red-head.
And me, with the best looking man anywhere.
I'll order pizza."

Dating for three-
Eating for two...

## ~ *Eighteen* ~

*T*here have been studies on how long it takes for redheads to be put to sleep. Not the "put to sleep", as in "my dog is really old" sort of put to sleep. I mean snoozing for tests of some sort like an MRI, or an MRA, or searching body parts with dyes.

Well, give the research its due. Whoever came up with the notion of separating easy sleepers from hard sleepers by their hair color had it down right. My red haired girl is not a knock out after all. She has a legendary reputation at Columbus Children's Hospital for fighting to stay awake even after all the drugs for downing a small elephant have been injected.

We watch her in amazement, rolling around, trying to get up, banging her head, and making noises like a goose on speed.

Why? What important thing will she miss if she just lets it take over and drifts off? It's like she's trying to win a bet she'll stay awake, and just when we think she has indeed won; she loses.

Then the race is on to see how much can get done while she's out cold. I used to request they do a couple of procedures while this opportunity of enforced cooperation exists; maybe find a dentist to check her teeth, or have the wax removed from her ears. But after wasting the time of perfectly good specialists on several occasions, I gave up asking. She wakes up before the first procedure is done.

Only the skill of the wonderful anesthesiologists at Children's kept Shelly asleep for her surgeries themselves. I have a couple of favorites. Dr. T. is tall, amazingly thin, the goodness from heart shining from his eyes, even when so late in the night those eyes are bloodshot and worn.

"How did you get here?" I hear him ask families

who are new to surgery. They usually tell him they drove.

"I can tell you this, your child will be safer with me than they were on the ride to the hospital." He tells them this, having learned over the years what a great comfort such a truth can be to a parent.

Of course, if you have been driving a lot in Columbus, you may think this is far from any promise of no problems, but it feels reassuring anyway.

My other favorite is a woman with hair even redder then my Shelly's. She always remembers Shell, always happy to see her again. They never seem too rushed, as busy as they are, to sit and answer questions and talk.

These people see many children in a day. Are they aware they have become part of our lives? Theirs are the faces remembered. Their words are the kindnesses remembered...

Columbus Don was never just a hospital volunteer. Before I ever met Michelle, as he always called her, he helped care for her. He rocked her and held her when no one else could do it. He fell in love with her and must have wondered if he would ever see her again when we first left the hospital for our home.

But God placed Don in our lives for good. Another foster mom, whose child he helped care for too, had nick-named him 'Columbus Don' and the name suited. Too often to recount, he made the time to give us a ride to and from the hospital.

He was there as a friend to sit in waiting rooms and worry along with me during surgeries Don acted as my 'stand-in' when I couldn't be there for Shell, filling me in on all the details of her time and taking pictures which I treasured.

But he also became Shelly's extended family while we were at home. He was the only one who remembered every birthday and sent cards to be read to her, or gifts for

her to open. Don was the one who made sure she was remembered on Christmas and often in-between times for no
reason at all. He would find a card reminding him of Michelle and send it with a note, or would write us long old-
fashioned letters. He was like a favorite uncle and she
searched for him during every hospitalization.

Some of God's angels are visible.

Many people at the airports, seeing the bulk of my
baggage and the child I was carrying would ask if they
could cart some luggage for me.

Even before 9/11, airport personnel wanted to know
if strangers had touched your bags, and I couldn't risk the
kind of delay it would put us in, so I always refuse the aid.

But I never forget, and will always appreciate, their
concern and desire to help. When I am with Shell, the
world seems to contain the most helpful and thoughtful
souls imaginable. Rarely do I return from our hospital trips
without stories of kindness.

Unwitting, unaware... Shelly brings out
Goodness.

## ~ *Nineteen* ~

- Shelly! Stop grinding!
You are driving me crazy!

- Tom, *please* tap her lips
to remind her not to grind.

- Why are you awake?
- Shell is grinding her teeth. I can't sleep...

~

- One of these days
she'll only have gums left.

~

- No, the phone is fine...
I'm holding the Bean and she's grinding.

~

- What is that noise?
- It's Shell. She grinds her teeth.
- Doesn't it drive you nuts?
- I don't even hear it anymore.

 

There are many reasons not to be foster or adop-
tive parents - many very good reasons. The world is full of
opportunities.

I'm glad to know while I'm fostering, there is someone else out there studying gorillas in the wild, or working
with the elderly, or rescuing dogs from the local pound.
Many people have care-giving built into their lives, with
birth children and elderly parents, without adding to the
mix.

But I hear from people who yearn to be foster parents and decide not to. Most often they tell me they
couldn't deal with eventually having the kids taken away,

their love for a child would be too great and they would hurt too much to separate.

Ah, but every child deserves to have someone in their lives who loves them enough to be devastated if they had to lose them. We want to be loved that much, to be missed that much, to have at least some honest tears shed at our funerals.

I think most of us can live through sorrow. We can survive separations. We can love without reserving a part of ourselves because we're afraid to hurt.

If we don't reach out when our hearts nag us to do so, we may deprive a child of love and a home and family, and we may deprive ourselves of an irreplaceable chance to grow.

Yes. I'm climbing off my soapbox...

Diarrhea hounded our lives from the very start. Shelly would have episodes lasting so long that we forgot what life was like without scooping poop. I could wake in the morning and know not only that she had loaded the bed, but what kind of diarrhea it was.

I'm betting you'd wish I don't describe—so I won't.

One bout began early in September of 1998 going and going (and smelling), strong, way into October. Naturally it made Shell cranky, and it kept me awake, up and down changing her all night - so cranky it was, all around.

In desperation for sleep one night, I took an over-the-counter sleep aid, wanting to get rest at any cost, but the feelings of guilt were stronger than the pill, and I kept myself awake all night, afraid I might not hear her.

And yet, we still gadded about as if we led the most normal of lives. Shell still went to school where they changed her often. We had church on Sunday mornings and went back again for bible study on Sunday evenings-

The 'Diarrhea Queen' went everywhere.

Surely, I was deranged.

One Sunday morning I tried to listen to the service as well as keeping the Broviac Brat from kicking the pew or climbing irretrievably under the pew, or chewing on the pew in any fashion, when I noticed it had gotten very quiet. They were preparing for communion and the usual pianists were absent.

So it seemed all the louder when Shelly reached over and entirely ripped off the long wooden hymn holder from the pew in front of us. One full-bodied angry grunt, the screech of nails reaming from the pew and she banged it to the floor!

Ah, my mortifying Redhead. We took our sorry selves home.

~ *Twenty* ~

There was a time
When the world was crazy.

Why tell of a time in our lives insane with comings and goings? It is, I suppose, everyone's life at some point.

With mornings so early they blended into the late night before. With eyes glazed over from lack of sleep - while teaching, while talking, while mowing grass, while driving - with meetings and clinics and newsletters and church and shopping and regular appointments and regular emergencies. With phone calls daily about home schooling, cancellations, changes in schedules, sleep-overs, medical supplies, lab work, and those from extended family. Phone calls - of marriages breaking up, weddings, sibling frustration, car accidents, surgeries, reminiscing, reminders and recriminations. With piano lessons, Toastmasters, violin lessons, gymnastics and regular visits to Granny in the nursing home. With pets growing old, pets dying, and new pets blending in. With worries about home and work and life and marriage and children and the future. With fears for extended family members - heart disease, Alzheimer's, alcoholism, pain circling lives and tearing at the fabric of peace... Well, you know... the usual.

But in addition to all this normal stuff, we constantly searched for an intervenor or respite.

The summer of 2000 - the summer without any help at all - I had searched every source I could think of from Canada to our own hometown for anyone even remotely interested in being an intervenor.

There was a woman who came recommended by Shell's teacher, and we began the process of long phone calls filled with details and explanations. From there we proceeded to house visits, and hours of teaching about the oddities of a child like Shell and finally reached the stage of 'when', 'where', 'how much'.

We picked a date for her to begin work, a hands-on daily time with Shell to keep her signing skills from eroding, to take her to interesting places like swimming and the park, and generally to let Shell and I have a life with a few hours a day apart.

We expected her to start on a Monday, but the phone call came the Friday before, saying she had changed her mind. She would be getting married soon and, "I need more time to prepare," and "I'm not sure I could communicate with Shelly." She feared dealing with Shell would be much more "complicated" than she had originally thought.

I deep-dove into depression after her call, but I should have prepared myself for this likelihood. She was not the first person, and as it turned out, not the last either, to do this. I would spend-and-waste hours and days of time preparing either for the intervenor position or a respite position involving IV hook-ups - people with good intentions- yet backing out at the last moment leaving me dazed and feeling forsaken.

Shelly was complicated - inside and out. She was very, very complicated, and I eventually began to refuse to train one more person into her life. I couldn't bear the thought of going over everything again and again in the hopes someone would actually work with her. Tom would hear of someone, a friend of a friend, a sister of a firefighter, a woman he'd met at clinic day, any female with no job and a viable pulse. He tried to help, desperate for relief and frustrated beyond words. We were so tied down, and he resented when I quit trying.

I, on the other hand, had nothing more to give - burned out from talk, burned out from teaching, burned out from disappointments. All this time had been wasted for nothing and I wanted to say, "Okay, you find the next person, you teach the next person!" I couldn't explain how much I wanted to be with him and have some normal life, but this was beyond me.

I also had some pretty well-founded fears about the kind of job another person would do with The Bean. Previously, a woman had been recommended as a caregiver for Shell by someone I trust. It appeared legit - a teacher's aide who wanted a summer job - and even though I felt uneasy with her ability to communicate in sign, I arranged with her to get Shell in the morning and do things with her during the day. My unease grew as the days and weeks of summer went on. I followed them as they left one morning, only to find them going to do a few errands and soon returning to the woman's trailer home and staying there for the day. I felt horribly guilty knowing Shell's time was wasted, and would have ended it right then and there but for an overriding guilt. The rest of my family needed me too.

A special child can change the dynamics forever in a family. All time must be negotiated. We would take shifts being with Shell or any of our other special needs children over the years - shifts to mow grass, to teach school and music classes, to run to errands, or on rough nights, even to sleep. We would make every effort to be there for our other children, fully aware of how kids can grow up filled with memories of coming in second in the lives of their parents. We hoped they would come to adulthood not feeling deprived, but learning a life can be rich in compassion and still have joy. We grabbed any free time available and took long hikes, brief canoe trips, overnight camping when we could. They didn't get a free ride through childhood, but perhaps a deeper experience than so many of their peers.

Our philosophy is—what is normal for your family is normal for your family.

## ~ Twenty One ~

*I* want to keep her busy - it's a long summer. I unhook her IV and we sit on the floor together as she picks out clothes to wear from the choices I put in front of her. She chooses her red t-shirt over her yellow one, sight unseen. She chooses her blue sneakers over her white ones; she happily stands as I put on her fanny pack and I sign to her that she is first going in the car, and then going to the store. She is excited and puts her palm to her chin, lifts her head and makes happy noises while informing the angels.

Every step out of the room is orchestrated with all her stops, turns, and motions. The choreography is precise throughout the rest of her journey to the car, clearing off counters, closing doors along the way, and tipping a pencil from the table to the floor, picking it back up good-naturedly when I tap her shoulder and insist. But her speed and purpose were energized by her mission and we soon get to the car, already hot in the summer morning sun.

She is buckled and starts rocking back and forth, as if to speed the car along, and I'm happy she's happy. Tom is working at the Station Two firehouse, and I decide to stop in with Shell for a surprise visit and extend our field trip. Did I mention it's a long summer?

I pull into the parking lot and get Shelly unbuckled. She jubilantly takes my arm as we walk to the side door. Her mood changes drastically as we step inside and she feels the front of Engine Two. She pulls aside trying to drag at me with no clear direction. I'm confused and bemused... or bemused and confused. The Bean has a mind of her own, and sometimes I find it hard to relate.

Tom finds us there, and sees Shell's indignation is building as she thrashes and pulls at her fanny pack, so he suggests she may want to sit in the fire truck, normally a celebrated pastime. She most assuredly does *not* want to sit in the fire truck. We lead her into the kitchen, and she is just as miffed to be there, rejecting the kindnesses of the firefighters on duty and pulls out her hearing aids. I manage to snatch them from her before they are ripped apart. I'm completely bewildered. My happy child disappeared so quickly.

There is no chance of a relaxing visit with Tom, so I gather up the remnants of the fanny pack from the floor, and the shreds of my parental dignity as we make our way back out to the car. I buckle her behind the driver seat, the side with the child proof door lock for safe keeping. Shell is red-faced with anger and now her rocking back and forth involves head butting on the seat and her noises are sharp and strident.

Now I debate. I told Shelly we were going to the store, and really need to pick up a few things, but as mad as she is, I'd be an idiot to even try another public appearance.

So, I'm an idiot. We pull out on the by-pass and head through heavy traffic toward the shopping center. I hear an unfamiliar noise and I scream when I glance back to see Shelly throwing herself across the bench seat and pulling the latch on the opposite door. It swings wide open as I swerve to pull off the road while loose tissues flutter into the wind...

The adrenalin rush, which seems to start in my hands and spreads in an instant to the rest of my body even before my scream ends, has me scrambling to get the car into 'Park' and I grab at my girl, somehow terrified she will escape her seatbelt and follow the tissues out the door. She is entirely unaware of my horror, managing to sit back up, assuming our stopping means we've arrived someplace. We stay where we are until my heart stops pounding quite so hard, and I can focus on the world again.

After re-checking the door locks, I look around and see we are near Walmart, so I pull into the parking lot, finding a spot near the door. The thought of driving right now appeals to me less than dealing with a fiery redhead in a store. It's come to that.

I get out of the car on my shaky legs and open the door for Shelly. She grabs my still trembling hands and insists on signing to me. She is not an aggressive signer, by any means, but in this case she has a message for me... "I go shopping! I go shopping!" This is a new one on me, and I have my doubts I've 'heard' her correctly.

We walk through the doors as they slide open before us, getting hit by cool air conditioning, and an older man in a blue vest offers us a shopping cart while attaching a smiley-face sticker to Shell's red Tee-shirt. She assumes a jaunty, 'I-told-you-so' air, and happily heads off into the store. Pealing the smiley face off and tossing it down before we reach the first aisle.

I am stunned by her change in behavior. I'm not a shopper and can't comprehend how one would willingly (and happily!) leave a perfectly good home, fight maniac traffic, circle a parking lot for a dubiously perfect spot, bustle through crowds of strangers (or worse yet, acquaintances) to spend money on stuff.

Everything about it drives me crazy. Pawing through clothes, subjective pricing, bras and underwear strategically placed so everyone shopping for gummy bears or shotgun shells will pass by and see you searching for your cup size.

"Hello, Uncle George. Yes, it's just me. Yes, buying a thong."

So, I'm here with Little Miss Headstrong Shopper and watch her march along with no sight or hearing. I'm won over. She makes me so proud my eyes brim with tears and I take her in the direction of toys, thinking she has earned

85

the right to a treat for her sheer determination that I stick to my promise of shopping. On the way, we pass bathing suits and I quickly see a possibility for her size and slip it into our cart. I don't pretend to think I could get her into a dressing room for a fitting, so I'll return it if we need to. Okay, I'll ask Tom to return it if we need to.

Passing by throw pillows, Shelly searches through with her hands until one feels right to her. She's delighted to discover a zipper along one edge and walks off with it, leaving me to pick up the discarded, uninteresting pillows and catch up when I can. She's practically humming.

I find the toothpaste I came for and quickly toss hand lotion and deodorant into our cart as we sail on past those useless items, and keep going until Shelly bumps into a shelf of wedge cushions for reading in bed. She dives into the lot and, dropping her zippered pillow, she unhesitatingly pulls one out, hugging it for a long minute and hauls it off. The check-out woman must lean over to find the tag with her wand when Shell won't let go. I decide to purchase the pillow too, and later, as Shelly searches our bags for it, I'm glad I did.

We ride home with happy sounds and locked doors. Did I mention this is a long summer?

## ~ Twenty-Two ~

Hours and hours in the tire swing-
Up and over,
Up and over again...
Safe in its cradling form is my Shell.

Feet tucked in, cross-legged
She soars, up and over,
As high as I can make it go –
Running underneath and pushing up.

She lets her brothers twirl her
Tight circles, giggling
Anticipation of when they will finally let go- and she
unwinds in a whirl...

Hours and hours in the tire swing-
Up and over again.


Sometimes I'm shaken to the core just watching
this child, feeling the weight of caring for something so
precious.

She's so brave I marvel at her. She gets up from the
chair, after sitting with me, and there is a decision made. I
don't know if she makes it when her feet hit the floor, or,
more likely, somehow and sometime before I sign to her to
get to bed. In that very second of standing upright, I know
which unalterable way she's chosen to go: to the couch for
her "chores" and then to bed, or to the rest of the house.
No amount of persuasion will get her to change her mind if
she's determined to go exploring.

I know what she wants. She wants something new

and interesting to take back to bed, but after years of nightly scanning the house, there's little left to find fitting the bill. It can't be soft, or small, or conventional. Often it is a binder, or a straight object like a ruler, but she gets tired of them too, and I've seen her reject them even when I point them out to her. I keep her in mind whenever I'm in a store, and have come home with new toilet plungers, odd clothes hangers, cookie sheets, zippered notebooks, and other unlikely toys, but even the stores run out of exciting objects.

Shelly will stand up, stop, check the recliner to be sure the footrest is in place, and to be sure it will swivel all the way around freely.  By this time I know she's heading out, and I turn off her feeding machine, and replace her tube connection with another drainage bag, so she'll be free to roam.

She heads out of her room, stopping to move anything she finds with her feet. When she reaches the door she stops to remove, with her right hand, her old knapsack from the hook, passing it back to me without turning around and waiting patiently if I'm slow to take it. If I were to find another spot for it, she would search and not be satisfied until it is found.

With her left hand, Shelly pries open the narrow plastic door of the tall shoe cabinet by the door, and leaves it wide open. As she goes through the door of the room, she pauses a moment, slams it behind her hard enough to hear or feel the vibration when it shuts, and turns herself in place, one revolution.

If I don't manage to slip out through the door before it closes, I wait, and the dogs wait patiently with me, while it shuts in our faces. Then I open it enough to slip through, closing it so she will not know her work was disrupted.

From there she skirts the wall to the right, and any chairs along it. Often there is something- a basket of un-folded clothes or a box of tools, and if I don't want her to rummage through them, I have to beat her to the punch, and remove them from her 'sight.'

The table is often in much better shape because of Shelly's nightly inspections. During the day I'm more in-clined to keep it cleared of items I care about because it's hard to stop a tornado in the evenings. If I've left some-thing precious, like my violin, sitting out, I have to fly over to save it before her small searching hands discover it and I must answer for its disappearance.

Shell forgets nothing. If Tom leaves his nice new binder with all the little pockets and interesting zippers, sitting on the table after he's used it to write a sermon, and Shell finds it for even the slightest moment, she has memorized what she likes about it, and nothing I can give her to replace it will do. She will grow angry if she can't find it, and won't give up looking until she's completely ex-hausted.

Leaving the table, she may check out the bench un-der the window, or the hutch, which is often a goldmine of treasures. Tom unloads his pockets there, and she loves to drop each coin to the floor, balancing it on the edge of the shelf, feeling it hit the ground. His wallet, reading glasses, cell phone and fire department pager are all fair game if I don't get there in time.

From the hutch, she makes her way into the kitchen, sweeping the right side first for any object out of place, or of new interest; a paintbrush, a salt shaker, a napkin. Most of the time, she leaves the bird cages alone, with only a casual, passing hand to checking for imperfections.

Getting to the stove I watch for anything new or still warm, and move whatever I can. She hands me everything else; the elephant tea pot, the vase of arrowhead plants rooting by the sink, the hand towels. As she gets to the left side of the sink, she changes tactics enough to insist on everything going into the sink, instead of tipping them to the floor, or handing them to me.

From there she crosses the room and starts on the opposite counter, which is notoriously interesting. This could involve a large stray onion, the days' mail and news-paper, a bag of dog treats, a thermos with a loose lid, a sling shot.

There is often much time spent here, balancing pens and dropping them to the floor, handing me a bag of chips, or a box of tissues, or a baseball cap. Everything she drops to the floor, she waits and expects me to tap her on the shoulder; and then she gets down, finding it and handing it up to me. Sometimes it's a long ritual.

Then we make our way back into the classroom, where she heads right to the bathroom door, which she can tell is left open. She opens it further, until it taps hard against the computer desk, and gives it a huge, satisfying slam shut. By this time I've tried to clear as much of the area around the computer as I can, pushing back the speak-ers and monitor to the far wall, putting the keyboard and mouse and all small items like coasters up on the printer and out of the way. Even Shelly abides by her own rules: only the desk is to be cleared. Anything on the printer or the pc tower is safe from harm. Rules are rules.

If Shell has found a new toy by this time, she turns to me with it safely and firmly in hand, and signs "up", wanting a lift to the bedroom. By then I'm happy to com-ply.

If The Bean finds nothing worthy of her devotion, she makes her way back to the room with me in tow. She clears the cushions from the couch, checks the recliner for hu-mans to pull off, or Belle the Golden to give a twirling ride to and lines herself next to the bedside. Like Dorothy in the Wizard of Oz, she turns around three times and reaches for me to lift her in, both of us exhausted.

~ * ~

*~ Laura Fitzmorris, Aunt ~*

*Shelly was the strongest person I know, and she's given me a lot to live up to.*

*She was a fiery redhead, half my size, but she could still beat me up.*

*Home for me is Aunt Claire's and Uncle Tom's. I'd been away longer before, but I was back for an evening movie-viewing with Aunt Claire. After the movie, it was time for Shelly to go to bed.*

*Like always, except when she decides to explore the house first, she headed for the couch to clear it off. This is her job. It is what she does every night. And I was sitting on the couch. I could have gotten up and out of her way. I've done it before when she hasn't felt well and doesn't need the distraction. But usually I just wait for her to find me. Because when she does, we hug.*

*This is my role with Shelly. Hugs. I like it. Even when they're perfunctory. Even when she really just wants me to get up off her couch.*

*But this night in particular, Shelly hugged me hard and long. I don't know when else I've felt so special.*

*~ \* ~*

We dance. I pick her up and we whirl around the room, hands clasped in ballroom position, twirling so often it no longer dizzies us. She throws her head back in glee and we both laugh.

I put on Irish music, and we dance far longer than I should have the strength to, spurred on by the beat. Her 80 pounds seems weightless until the music is finished and we flop exhausted on the recliner.

Other times I take her small hands in mine and we move in rhythm, her feet on the floor, playing along with me as if she can hear the music. We take turns twirling up under our joined arms, and I dip her low to the ground. She's enraptured and I'm enchanted, ready for more...

Dancing with angels in heaven must be like this.

## ~ Twenty-Three ~

What should be done with someone who just refuses to go along with the system? What do you do with someone who always balks at school authority and the way things "should" go? What do you do with someone who gets so frustrated when they can't make themselves understood?

And it's not just me - Shelly is like that too!

I guess part of why I home schooled my kids had something to do with my inability to play well with the system. But Shell needed to be in school, so I needed to be nice, even when I didn't feel nice.

Dress codes meant wearing a shirt with a collar—but Shell found collars intolerable. She pulled them until they ripped apart; she fought tooth and nail with them if they didn't rip. Finally the school made an exception. Shell wore tee shirts - everyone was happier.

I loved Shell's teachers and intervenors, but spent many hours over the years grumbling in long harangues played out in my mind, if I thought they were wrong, or if the system came before my Shelly.

At one point I strongly disagreed with how she was expected to learn. She got daily lessons for the following:

- Sign language by a combination of English, ASL and gross motor signs in her hands.

- Voice with the hearing aids for any pitch she might hear.

- Braille in small, medium and large dots.

- Finger spelling.

- And the final straw for me: the alphabet in raised letters.

Enough already!

Shelly's boredom was a big reason for her unhappiness in school and for her acting-out while there. Everyone had a different, confusing direction for her. When notes and reports drew me into this system against my will, I rebelled along with her, but I had the advantage of words and Shelly did not. Most of my words stayed at home, but occasionally the system would request my active participation.

Once, I was asked to write up a paper, telling what things Shell and I did at home to demonstrate her 'turn-taking' and perhaps also discuss some 'choice-making' activities.

Too cynical to be sent, the first letter let me break into absurdity:

*"I am writing concerning some turn-taking games in which Shelly partakes at home. She does not initiate these games, but seems to enjoy them when we begin them with her (i.e. force her to play).*

*In truth, Shelly is only a pawn in my 'games of life' and we find her involuntary participation to be hilarious. She hates the games and I am beginning to suspect she actually hates us for making her play them, but no matter. We carry on. How long does this letter have to be? Does it have to have a point? Will I cause Shelly to flunk out of public school if I fail to write this? Is it getting hot in here?*

*So. Turn-taking. Occasionally, I will throw the cat at Shelly and she throws it back at me, and I throw it back at her, and she throws it back at me. Maybe I'm saying too much about myself here.*

*Another turn-taking occurs when we dance. At times I lead, at times she leads. Is this a good example?*

*While you catch me in such a letter writing mood, I think I will also go into Shelly's choice-making at home. Don't settle in, it's not a long story, but it does have its moments.*

*In the realm of what is important, Shelly has almost no choice about anything. For that matter, we are all pretty limited in most respects; where we are born; genetic make-up, who our parents are, whether or not we will fall for a guy who will be bald in twenty years...*

*But leave aside 'to be or not to be' choice making - (Shelly may not have picked deaf/blindness) In the little matters, we all like to feel we have some choices, which believe me, blue eye shadow should not be one of them.*

*At home, Shelly can help to choose her clothes, for instance. Makes no-never-mind to her if the tee shirt is blue or green, but she may like to wear sneakers instead of hiking boots or sandals. She may want shorts instead of blue jeans.*

*She can have a fake sense of making these choices, because I'm not going to present her with anything I can't live with. She would always go to school in her bathing suit if she had free range. Also, when we are late for church, Shelly is compelled to wear whatever comes to (my) hand quickly.*

*C'est la vie.*

I really am normal... on the outside.

I believe the final draft had some calmed-down affair of:

*I am writing concerning the turn-taking opportunities Shelly has at home. We often play catch when an extra person can help Shelly with the actual catching part. She anticipates the ball coming, with her hands held out, and throws it in some direction to return it.*

*The dogs join in this play from time to time, and this is amusing to Shelly, although she is a bit more reluctant to pull a slimy, smelly, disgusting, drool-covered ball from their mouths to continue the game.*

*Sincerely, (at last),*
*Claire Muller*

And school... They had classes, they had vacations, they had 'in-service' days, they had early let-outs, they had snow days, they had 'what-if-it-snows-days'. They had lice causing time out, flu causing time out, holidays causing time out. All of this made sense to everyone but Shelly. She liked routine.

She didn't comprehend things changing, and had such limited stretches of feeling good, she'd often end up too ill to be in class when it was in session, and felt healthy at home when it was not.

I kept trying to outwit the system by getting the other system - social services - to help provide money for her intervenor to work when the schools were closed. Even if she stayed at home with someone teaching her, she could have some consistency. But inevitably, the intervenors became part of the school, and were involved in the meetings and happily anticipated the breaks.

There is no perfect system...

Shell had long since taught me to not view her life in line with what the rest of the world did, so when I got a note from her school saying I needed to write an 'excuse' note for Shell's absences I never gave it another thought. I figured they were referring to children whose absence was unexpected, or unusual, or at least not observed first-hand by her intervenor—a school employee in constant contact with us.

So it took some time before I picked up on a bizarre reality. Miss Shellybeanie would end up in detention or possibly be expelled if I didn't get writing these notes.

I'm assuming there is some sort of *Note Auditor* who Goes from school to school and checks off names on an absentee paper and matches their name to a handwritten note from home, or a signed slip from the doctor. I wondered if this *Note Auditor* actually read the notes, so I would write them in hopes of livening up her/his day.

For instance:

*Dear Note Auditor,*

*The case of the missing Michelle Thurman has been solved, and the mystery is now to be revealed. On Thursday last, while not appearing in her normal class, Michelle was, in fact, being held (against her will) under her covers, flu-like symptoms being at the bottom of it all.*

*Friday, looking none the better, she was spirited away to her physician, who pronounced her Viral, (Something we've long suspected.)*

*Alas! Monday - a veritable holiday - and there is a reprieve from explanations.*

*Tuesday still held Michelle in the tailend of her fevers, and the decision to retain her at home was made. So, there she was, retained.*

*Wednesday, with the full bloom of health upon her cheek, she returned to her education, surely to the cries of joy from all the welcoming assembly of faculty and students.*

*What fears and trepidations must have struck the hearts of all, when expecting her eminent return on Thursday, she failed to appear at the appointed time. More illness, a recurring malady, possibly infectious to the general school population, perchance requiring some sort of evacuation and quarantine?*

*No! No! Such was not the case.*

*By an act of nature, by the torrential down-pouring of rain, the child was detained by only two fearful hours! Water coursed over the bridge - should we risk crossing, or would we be cast into the raging stream, only to wind up peering up at a houseboat in the Kentucky River? Alas! A chance we did not take - and so Michelle was late. Today, there is no mystery as to Michelle's whereabouts. She is safely in the confines of her class, and anyone wishing to verify this may, of course, do so.*

*Sincerely,*
*Claire Muller, Shelly's mom*


The day Shelly's report card came in, and I discovered she had achieved an 'A' in Science and Technology, but had been given an 'F' in Life Skills, I'm afraid I was at the limit of my comprehension.

An 'F' in Life Skills? Shelly? Really?

This is a child to whom there could be no high enough grade in Life Skills.
This is a child who, without fearful expectations or holding grudges, suffered needles, operations, prodding and pain.
This is a child who brought life to every denied opportunity without complaint of her misfortunes.
This is a child who could find joy in the smallest moments of a small life and bring it to others who had their eyes open.
This is a child who was given boredom and rebelled heroically.
This is a child who, at every turn, denied death and lived.
Don't give me a report saying this child gets an 'F' in Life Skills.
I raised the roof, charging *foul*!
They changed the report card - the one Shelly would never read or know about.
Noted: Did not attend Life Skills.
Ah, the System.

## ~ Twenty-Four ~

Long gone is the fallacy, pretending Mother's Day is for Mothers. My first-ever Mother's Day was idyllic. Our best friends took us out for lunch at a nice restaurant, a lovely treat, and I got cards and flowers.

At the time, I was pregnant with my first child, barely showing and past the morning sickness stages, a happy fact leaving me free to revel in this stage of motherhood. It also completely misled me about how this holiday would be celebrated once the baby is born and henceforth...

How was I to know as I laughed and chatted at the table, napkin unsoiled with baby vomit, resting on my slightly showing belly - everything under the sun changes when the baby has actually been born?

How was I to know, as I enjoyed the entire meal without getting up to ask a waiter for a mop, or blubbering an apology to a nearby table for flying food, that my soft life was almost over?

From then on with unfailing regularity, Mother's Day has been a Mothering test of some sort. Over the years, I came to believe this day was designed to separate the Prizefighters from the Pretenders, the Glamour from the Guts, and the 'Aught-to-be-Committed' from the Uncommitted.

Mother's Day: A test of one's sang-froid and sanity.

For me, Mother's Day often began the night before, with a call from social services, and all the flurry of having a new foster child in the family. There is no rhyme or reason why it would be one particular weekend, but foster moms don't deal in 'rhyme or reason'. Before dawn there would likely be a vomiting child, or dog, or husband, to start the "Day."

With the expectation of church attendance, and the

manic activity normally accompanying, I could anticipate a broken dryer, socks without mates, (mates without mates - when Tom was working), over-sleeping kids, cranky kids, crying kids and lost keys. And this is just the morning.

With Shelly, I also found it to be the day for emergency rooms, repairing torn Broviac lines, bailing the overflow from a sabotaged water bed, or just plain exhaustion from an active night.

Mother's Day.
Happy Mother's Day to you!

## ~ Twenty-Five ~

*"C'est le temps que tu as perdu pour ta rose qui fait ta rose si importante."*
*(Le Petit Prince)*

Sometimes, you know the very moment your life changes forever. It may be a car accident, a house fire, a death. From then on you think in terms of 'before' and 'after' the event—sort of like the feeling we all had about 9/11. What we had considered normal would never be 'normal' again.

Other times, you know only by looking back and finding, through a series of events, how your world has been rocked.

November 5, 2001 began the series of events in our lives, changing us, and how we lived, for many years. It started with an occlusion in Shell's IV line. This was not an unheard of event, but of more concern as she was, by this time, depending on Picc lines instead of deep-line Broviacs.

Picc lines are peripherally inserted lines, used instead of deep-lines to the subclavian or jugular veins which are more easily infected. In Shell's case, we were using the Picc lines as a last resort, because her deep-lines were blocked up with scarring. We had been utilizing Piccs for over a year, wearing them out one at a time.

I found I couldn't even draw up blood cultures, so I called Becky Hoagland at Children's and she said we may have to bring her in the next day. That night I got little sleep, worrying about Shelly and also about leaving home. It was Tuesday, and my son Isaiah had a big concert coming up on Friday. He and some firefighters from our town were renting the theater to play music, raising money to send aid to families of NYC firefighters lost in the terrorist attack. I really wanted to be there to support him because this was too big to miss. Oh, the impossible guilt of motherhood.

Tom was on duty at the fire department the next day, so getting ready was all up to me. I called the hospital and made arrangements, called the airlines for flight times and tickets, called Shell's intervenor, Becca, and told her we'd be missing school, called my violin students and canceled them for the week, called social services and told them we were leaving and we may be needing a fax for permission to operate. I called Columbus Don and told him we'd be coming to the hospital for a few days.

Then I cleaned the house to the point of 'presentable', finished hemming a pair of pants for my daughter Shonta, packed a variety of things in as small a bag as possible, played my violin, got Shell packed and ready - aware of the new regulations for carry-on items,  and was ready to leave at ten-forty in the morning.

It was so hard to say 'goodbye' to Isaiah once again, and I rashly promised him I'd be home for his concert somehow. He was sweet enough to sound like he was just the right amount of sorry about my leaving.After all - he was almost sixteen and getting the house to himself, and probably not too sorry about it.

Having no idea how long our stay in Columbus would be, I stopped at the bank with Shell and withdrew $150.00. It seemed like a lot of money, but there would be cab fares and food and pull-ups of the type Shelly tolerated. I dropped off some overdue movies and drove the jeep to Lexington, pulling into the long-term parking lot with time to spare.

Shell walked for several yards, but easily wore out. She was dehydrating, having gone overnight without her lines working and I carried her the rest of the way. I had bags over one shoulder, pulling a suitcase on wheels, and eighty-five pounds of redhead; very grateful for the kindness of the Delta folks helping us through the lines and the security people who knew us well, offering assistance.

Two flights later we landed in Columbus and got a cab to the hospital. I answered all the driver's questions I could understand, nodding at those I didn't and murmuring things I hoped would suffice as his pleasant eyes reflected constant nodding in the mirror.

They were prepared for us in admissions and after a few signatures with the help of a squirming child on my lap, we went up to 4-Tower South. I was happy to have Amy and Betsy, who put in a peripheral line and managed to get in a urine catheter when it seemed hopeless.

Finally, Shell's Picc line was pulled out. There it was... another of those moments in a series of life changers.

*"But what does that mean - 'ephemeral'?*
*Repeated the little prince.*
*"It means, 'that which is in danger of quickly disap-*
*pearing.'"*
*"Is my flower in danger of 'quickly disappearing'?"*
*"Certainly it is."*
*(Le Petit Prince)*

The next morning came early with a host of familiar faces - those who have loved Shell over the years. Dr. King came to say they would go in for an MRA on the upper chest, looking for any open veins. I could see he didn't feel very confident of finding one, but he's the best and if anyone could, it would be him.

I hoped someone had taped the early morning show Isaiah's band was going to be on, promoting the concert. Already I felt like I'd missed out. (After a time in the hospital, or probably jail for that matter, one gets used to the alternate universe they are going to be in, but in the be-Ginning there is much tearing back and forth, living in two

102

worlds.)

Our son Nathan, and his college sweetheart, Dana, were getting married soon and I spent much of the day stitching a design on gift pillowcases. I kept busy while waiting for Shell to be called down for her MRA. When it got late, Betsy called and found out they had put Shell down for a late time slot.

Techs who didn't know her thought she wouldn't need drugs to lie still - "since she was a fifteen-year-old." Her nurses and I had a laugh, trying to picture Shelly cooperating with anyone about lying down quietly! So, it got put off until the morning and I gave the Bean a bath, while Betsy held her arm out of the water, preserving her precious small IV line.

I didn't sleep too poorly, for a night in the hospital, and we were up early the next morning, feeling rushed but wanting coffee badly enough to risk missing the intern's visit. As it was, he didn't have any new information, but Dana, our favorite male nurse, called and found the MRA once again set for seven o'clock p.m.

Upset, but in hopes of somehow making it to Isaiah's concert, I called the car rentals at the airport and reserved a vehicle for the next day. I thought if I kept moving forward as if it would happen, I would make it to the concert... I would make it to the concert.

In the evening when we went down for the MRA, I heard they were planning to do a head scan first, and I protested. No matter how much the doctors and nurses and technicians know, a Mama still has to speak up. I knew how hard it was to keep Shelly asleep, and the vein scan was the most important fact-finding mission of the night. They switched it for me, and as I'd thought, Shell we up just as the venous scan ended.

Back up in the room a doctor came by to say they

would let us know in the morning if her surgery would be tomorrow but it was certain to be late afternoon. I was torn, knowing I'd have to miss being there for one of my kids—either Shell or Isaiah—I fell asleep crying.

I rose by five o'clock the next morning, skipping coffee in fear of missing the doctors. I was always on alert in the hospital, no matter how often I stayed there. I would marvel at other parents wandering down to get breakfast in their pj's and sleeping soundly through the morning rituals. I've always felt somehow sleep is a guilty pleasure and would wear a pair of sweats to bed, or even sleep in my jeans, so I could spring up looking 'awake for hours'.

Dr. Kwan came by with no news, the surgery team standing outside our door without entering. Finally, I caught up with Dr. King in the hall and he took the time to draw on a board the "disastrous" lower and left veins of Shell's sweet heart. He said he would try to thread up and around a block in the right subclavian, or through the hepatic vein as a final attempt at a deep line.

I stood there, grateful for his honest and frank nature and tried to somehow connect in my mind the sentence he had just given out - sort of a life sentence with a chance at parole.

I must have been tired enough, or my mind was frantic enough, because I told this man, whom I admired to the point of awe, my dilemma of staying with Shelly or getting back for Isaiah's concert.

"Go - I'll work on her this afternoon and take good care of her." He looked at me kindly. About half an hour later, the transport team came up and said a patient was going to come in late and Dr. King had switched Shelly to that spot. Relief overwhelmed me.

They could only get a few drops of blood for her preop work-up, but as her hydration was only going to worsen as time went on, it was now or never. They took her in at eleven-forty in the morning.

I watched Shell being wheeled away, not knowing it would be the last time I would have to go through that particular agony - the agony of standing in the hall, the air leaving your lungs, your heart trailing the gurney as it rounds a far corner, knowing you can't do a thing more than leave it to God and the doctors.

Quickly, I found a phone and called my friend Chantel, whose husband, Danny, had offered to drive me to the airport, and I arranged the time for one o'clock p.m. Then I went to the waiting room, nerves jarring every time the in-house phone rang.

When it was finally for me, Dr. King told me gently they had no luck getting a vein and I could come into recovery to see her. Poor miserable Shelly - she had two new cuts, one in front and one in back, and no comfortable position. I tried everything I could to soothe her. The staff in recovery was familiar with her from many years of surgeries, and gave her enough morphine to make her comfortable and let her sleep, reassuring me they would take good care of her.

I had to leave then or not go at all. Danny came and met me upstairs, and by the time we got into his car, he must have wished to be anywhere else on earth but next to this inconsolable weeping woman - I was a mess beyond speaking and he was kind beyond compare.

Danny and his dad both ministered at the Hilliard Church of Christ, a dynamic congregation of caring Christians in Columbus. I know Danny's family to have dealt with more than most when it comes to physical ailments, and he came for me that day, sent by God, with the understanding born of experience. I was emotionally and spiritually distraught, and he handled it with the calm and caring I needed right then.

At the airport I got my rental and the drive home took four hours. It was a nail-biter for me – what with all the crying at first, then the realization I was the only driver and I'd better stay awake, then passing two very bad accidents. There was no relaxing until I got to Winchester and pried my fingers from the wheel.

Quickly, I ran into the house for a much needed bathroom break, grabbed a cap for my head in lieu of brushing my hair out, bear-hugged the dogs, who were at first ecstatic to have me home, then morose as I took off for the theater downtown. I got there before it began, adrenalin-charged and exhausted at the same time.

The concert was great. There was a good crowd, the band really got everyone going, and Isaiah was amazing. I was glad to be there, but most of all, glad I'd kept my promise. In any family with multiple children, events conflict, we just do the best we can. But after all the focus for so long on Shelly, this concert seemed important not to miss.

While raising our children alongside all manner of other children, we did do a lot of things: a trip to DC, Gettysburg, the many trail walks and canoe excursions, enough camping to give them fodder for stories of growing up.

But we very often had to miss out on the impromptu 'let's-grab-a-bite-and-a-movie,' or those Road Trips we'd fantasized about doing with them as we home schooled. Everything outside of our routine involved respite, or lack of respite. And respite involved training, organizing, shuttling, more training, packing for kids going to a respite home, as well as packing for our trips. We reserved that kind of frantic, exhausting, overwhelming effort for things like Family Camp.

Later, I had trouble sleeping. I wandered around the house, grateful and sad, missing my Bean.

## ~ *Twenty-Six* ~

*"My flower is ephemeral,"* the little prince said to
himself, *"and she has only four thorns to defend herself
against the world. And I have left her on my planet, all
alone!"*

(Le Petit Prince)

*I* got back to the hospital around noon the next
day, to find they had moved Shell to a room across from
the nurse's station. She looked wonderful and seemed con-
tented, taking away some of the guilt I felt over leaving her
fresh from surgery.

The staff had found a soft sided 'cage' crib for her,
to keep her from escaping but still not making her look like
she was in a zoo. I unzipped the side and touched her soft
cheek. She acted as if she'd been expecting me. I held her
and rocked her, telling her about my adventures and singing silly songs until she fell asleep. Shell being deaf was not
a deterrent to my chatter.

The next day was Sunday, and the valleys were
deep. I couldn't seem to connect with anyone in the area
churches to get communion brought in, and there were too
many medical things pulling at my mind, so I didn't persist
like I should have.

I was told there was a woman doctor in Boston who
was good at finding veins when no one else could. Sometimes "good" news is all the more disheartening, because
reality causes overwhelming decisions to be made.

Hearing of this doctor, should we pursue such a
course? We have wonderful doctors here, and I have all the
faith in the world Dr. King would find a vein if there was
one. If we head to Boston - which is not next door - would
we have to go there for follow-ups even if she found a

107

vein? Would the state pay for it, and would the chance be worth the risk, knowing in time she would inevitably lose every usable vein?

Medically fragile children come with moral dilemmas, an interesting part of our amazing advances in medicine and science. With every life saved, or prolonged, we have new challenges of how to deal with what we save.

My grandparents lost their nine-month-old daughter with Spina Bifida. In those days, little could be done and my grandparents sorrowed for her the rest of their lives. My daughter, Shonta, was born with Spina Bifida. By the time we adopted her as a two-year-old, she had had several life-saving surgeries on her back, as well as a shunt inserted from her brain to drain excess fluid. What a difference in life expectancy by then.

Being the mom of many children whose lives were extended by new medicines, ground-breaking surgeries and therapies, I've been involved in interesting discussions about the benefits and drawbacks to this brave new world, and have given it much thought. My thoughts are 'tainted' by my faith in God, and His control over every situation, so I can only come from that point of view.

There is a strong element who would wish to choose. They would if possible, view the unborn child's errant genes, test his mind for retardation, scan his body for flaws, and decide to let him live or not. I would ask who they are saving and what they are losing by doing this. Is it a 'mercy' as some would suggest? To whom is it a mercy, the child or the caregivers?

Before I could ask those questions, I had to acknowledge not everyone is able to deal with what they were not expecting. I can't see into the heart of every situation, but having taken children for almost thirty years for those who were overwhelmed, I ask anyway. There may be someone able to love each child.

Nothing comes without consequence, good or bad.

The unborn child has no say in his or her conception. The consequence for conception may be unbridled joy
- or fear, misery and anger. Still, the consequences should
not rest on the child; the womb should not be a proving
ground for the unborn - if there were bad genes, rape, lack
of finances, or no husband – still, not the weight to be carried by someone so short.

Will there be pain and suffering? Every child kept
brings some sort of pain and suffering, even along with joy.
Every child aborted will bring loss and regret, suffering indeed, and without the added joy.

To the tune of a song, 'I feel sorry for anyone who
isn't me tonight!' I always sing, 'I feel sorry for anyone who
doesn't have Michelle!' And yes, we both have had pain
and suffering - years of hospitals, doctors, home health,
hospice, special school meetings, and special teachers.

She endured operations and medicines, and I missed
out on too many family events, and impromptu occasions,
to even count. But that is not what we lived... it's only
what we lived *through*.

We lived joy, and inexpressible possibilities of patience, compassion and love. We lived understanding, and
the incomparable chance to pass understanding on to the
rest of our children. We lived learning—learning about ris-
ing above adversity with grace, learning to cherish things
that matter above the petty, learning how to deal with situations and people - those who stare and avoid - those who
humble us with their help. We lived growth—growth we
didn't even know we wanted to have until we found ourselves on the other side and would never have wanted it
otherwise.

I'm happy for families who never have to deal with
an unexpected, or even a chosen, difficulty. But I feel sorry
for them too.

Not many people will get an 'easy-out, and avoiding
parts of life because they may cause you pain, or loss, or

sorrow, will not lend you strength for when you can't avoid them anymore.

## ~ Twenty-Seven ~

*K*wan Chun's father said when you use the Chinese letters, his name means 'Fortitude', or something like it. And his brother's name would mean 'Truth', which is nice. "But", he added, "I'm Korean and in Korean, my name means "Coffin.""

Oh well.

That is the kind of thing I find out while waiting in Shelly's hospital room hour after hour, day after day. I talk with every doctor and nurse about Shell, but sometimes they are only in there to check on something in her file, or as a student, or wandering past.

So I, desperate for diversion, grill them. I find out whose brother plays jazz in a nightclub every chance he gets; what the unlucky spelling for the Irish name Siobahn is; I learn who is married and how many children they have, and who lives with a boyfriend. I find out who is a stickler for the rules, who goes to what church, and how people spend their days off.

We form a hospital family.

I don't know what I'd do without loved ones calling and visiting. Tom's brother Ken, who lives near Columbus, came, sometimes with his family, and got me to laugh, no matter how hard the day.

My sister, Jean, phoned, and we talked until our ears hurt. My brother, John, and I could pick up on each other from all the miles away and know when we needed to connect. Nathaniel would call and catch me up on his life, and the church he worked for sent flowers. Isaiah called, sometimes twice a day, so I kept up with his recitals or how piano and violin lessons were going. Shell's teacher, Nancy Donta called regularly, as did Becca.

But my main-line drug of phone-choice was my

Tom. He knows every change in my mood, every inflection in my voice. When he told me I was "deteriorating" we both knew what he meant. I wasn't getting enough sleep, and was worrying myself sick.

I was walking the balancing rope of depression and crying more tears than I thought possible of producing. I was lonely. I was afraid for Shell's future. I was tired, tired, tired. Sometimes, I'd have to sit down just to keep from falling over.

But I knew I was where I should be, and Tom knew he was where he should be, too. We were doing what parents do when a child is sick. We loved each other from a distance and knew we were okay. We depended on God for the rest.

At night, Tom had prayer with me over the phone and it brought relief knowing we aren't ultimately in charge of anything.

On Monday, we spent the morning in Radiology with some very nice technician people. They allude to possibilities. The possibilities of a collateral vein, or of a 'ballooning' vein, or finally, procedures leaving her bedridden for good. I'm aghast at even the thought of such a thing, so little did I yet know of what one may bear in life.

Upstairs, I give the stinker a bath and she loved it—warm water, bubbles, clean hair—but she tires very quickly. She's really not gotten any nutrition since last Tuesday and was kept NPO (nothing by mouth, or in Shell's case, nothing by G-tube) all day because of the seven o'clock p.m. surgery.

That surgery never materialized as it becomes increasingly clear how limited our options are. There was even some speculation of a bowel/intestine transplant, but getting any IV line into Shell, even a peripheral one just for surgery is quite out of the question.

One of her doctors came in and sat for a long time-with me, talking about the present situation and asked if I have strong beliefs.

How do you answer such a question when the truth is you live on the very air of strong beliefs? To just say, "Yes, I'm a believer" or "I'm a Christian" sounds as trite as to seem a very betrayal of how wrapped your whole life is - in the knowledge and dependency of God and his grace. Somehow, the middle of such a conversation would convey my thoughts far better than the beginning.

I answer her by talking about Shelly, the closest human I know to the heart of angels.

What I know about Shell's Soul and Spirit is much more than doctors were ever meant to know about Shell's ailments. Those two parts of her are healthier than most of us wearing 'healthy' bodies, so who is really better off?

I picture Shell when I read of Jesus presenting the child to the apostles, with this type of innocence. I tell the doctor that I'm content with my present time with Shell, whatever it holds, and won't ask for what could be in the future.

Little did I know then how soon the stretch into my own soul and spirit would make all the days and years I'd lived before seem like a child's first steps.

Shell woke up a bit cranky on her sixteenth birthday. It is the day I will think back to in the years to come as the day I realized she was out of veins. In truth, she didn't have any major tests then, but I was finally grasping what the results of the day before in Radiology really meant. From this birthday on, our lives would change.

Amy, Shell's nurse who was a day away from her own birthday, brought in a new school binder for the redhead to happily play with. But what really made Shell laugh her deep-down-belly-laugh was when a neurologist stopped by with his little hammer and tapped her knees. Now that's the kind of gift my Bean loved.

The deaf kid also got calls from Columbus Don and

Stacey, and late at night, a sweet call from my sister, Jean, who played *Happy Birthday* on the piano—loving Shell, loving me.

The next morning came too early with a four o'clock a.m. bed change for Shell, then a five o'clock loud, boisterous voice of the dad in the next room. Forget sleep. I headed downstairs for coffee.

Anxious as I was to call Tom and wish him a *Happy Birthday*, maybe my gift to him would be to let him sleep later than I was able to.

Around ten o'clock, I stretched out on the couch to read my Bible. Shell's bed webbing kept me from seeing clearly to the door, when I heard a rap and familiar voice. It sounded like Tom's brother Ken, back for yet another visit.

"Are you accepting any visitors today?" the voice said, and my heart jumped to the sound of my Tom! This is *exactly* what the man I married would do! We stood kissing in the doorway for a long time, unmindful of where we were.

Tom had left home about six o'clock a.m. because the person he wanted to spend his birthday with was me. We sat and talked as he held Shelly, who was less impressed with his arrival than I. It was a relief to see the fresh clothes he brought me, and I changed my jeans right away.

I've met many families who have been with their children for months and this is their way of life, living from one change of clothes to another, not really remembering what "normal" is anymore. We are not exceptional.

In the afternoon our dear Doctor Murray came in to talk with us about Shelly. He stayed for a long time, and we discussed the Boston option, a risky heart medication being tested, and what it would be like to take Shelly home on only G-tube feeds.

The G-tube seemed to be our only reacl choice, and it would most likely end with her dehydrating from diarrhea and having to be given long rests if she was retching constantly. The end for her seemed so very near that I shook inside as I tried to stay calm outwardly.

When Dr. Murray left us, we got Shell as comfortable as we could and headed to the cafeteria for a meal before Tom would leave. On the way we stopped to talk with Dr. Mousa, who said she'd like them to attempt another line, but they'd not be able to fit her in before the next day.

Okay. It will be a try, and at least I would know we did what we could. They've always been able to find a vein, and Shell always surprised the doctors, so let's do it. Unfortunately, the plan also included Shell being much more hydrated than she was at present.

As I medicated her later through her G-tube, she was unable to even tolerate that much. We had to disconnect her as she retched uncontrollably.

The following day was Thursday, and I was coming undone after the ten day hospital stint. I had been in with her longer in the past, but this time, the stress made me ill and almost too depressed to speak. I had little appetite and slept poorly, overwhelmed with the thoughts of losing Shell in such an awful way. The plans for her were changing hour by hour and nothing seemed in the least bit hopeful. The next day would be Isaiah's sixteenth birthday and it looked like I'd miss being home. My head and ears were aching, and I was so dizzy, I assumed I'd gotten some sort of inner ear infection.

Shell was a mess. I was a mess.

I just wanted to go home.

Perhaps with this weakness I needed to feel some control over something in my life, so I called the airlines and reserved a flight for the next day, early afternoon. It was irrational, but somehow taking that step gave me some peace. I took the opportunity while Shell slept to do a detailed sketch of her, and when she woke up, I gave her a fun bubble bath. Her diarrhea worsened, yet her stomach got harder and distended.

Okay – Saturday, a flight for early afternoon - my *final* stand. I'm going, and I'm taking Shelly with me. Tom was getting worried since I could barely speak on the phone, depression storming in like the tide.

Heading to the store later for pull-ups, I met with another doctor who asked what I thought of the situation. I said I didn't know what the situation was. He said the situation of Shell not tolerating her feeds.Oh yeah—*that* situation. My mind was numb. The doctor said a line would go in tomorrow and she could go home.

"What if they can't find a line?" I asked. He looked at me for a moment.

"We'll have to talk, if that's the case."

My mind muddled around in frustration, panic, worry and exhaustion. I said nothing, but thought, *I don't think so. I'm leaving. Tomorrow. Morning. So talk. Now. Fast.*

I was glad to see Dr. Murray when I got back to Shelly's room. After a quick hug I sat down fast, not feeling well and lightheaded. He said that I didn't look so great. I told him about my ultimatum. I'd be leaving on Saturday with Shelly, and could she be *fixed* by then?

## ~ Twenty-Eight ~

November 16th came and with it, the heavy thought of missing Isaiah's birthday. Tom promised to take him to Lexington's Singletary Center to hear the Russian Favorites. It made me feel better - my coming home would be minor compared to listening to live Russian music.

Shell was drenched when she woke up. Her G-tube leaked from pressure, and her diarrhea was out of control. Still, when Radiology came for her late in the morning, she laughed all the way down on the gurney.

The radiologist found what he hoped was a small vein in her right foot. Then he came out to the waiting area and talked with me about the three possible veins they had picked up on. He seemed quite confident, drawing a picture for me to see, and causing me to gasp when one of the veins looked to be in the center of her throat.

I wasn't allowed to stay with her, so I waited, praying and yet not sure what to pray for. At first, as he seemed so sure, I pictured us going home with a new line, for as long as it would last and going through this again in the future. I tried but failed, to imagine Shell allowing a line to stay in her throat. They worked on her for a very, very long time, so when they came out to tell me Michelle was out of veins, I already instinctively knew, and said nothing.

I managed to keep myself in-check until we got upstairs to her room and closed the door. Then I cried until I could cry no more.

When Shell fell asleep I left her to find Amy in the nurses' room. She looked upset and it flashed through my mind that bad news travels fast. Reading what she was writing on the information board, I saw her distress was from another child. A boy named Joshua had just died.

"What now?" she asked, seeing my red eyes.

I didn't have the heart to tell her. I stammered condolences for the loss of this little boy and went back to Shell.

Those nurses at Columbus Children's—is there any way to tell them how much they meant to Shell and me all those years?

The love...

The love...

The love...

You can teach the other things - how to 'nurse': the measurements, the medications, the ritual of notes to the clipboard, the procedures. But you can't teach the love. And when the love is there, it makes all the technical stuff work better.

When Shell would come in, honestly too sick to survive, they would watch her as closely as if she were in the Intensive Care Unit.

"Shelly will *not* die on *my* watch," each of them said.

As a parent, those words reassured me like no others, even knowing perhaps they may be found false. But seeing Shell would have the best care possible because their hearts were completely hers. Hour after hour, attentive, questioning, supporting, and loving. Such is the legacy of those nurses at Columbus Children's.

And Shell did *not* die on their watch.

Becky Hoagland came in and explained a J-G tube in full detail. I had heard briefly about it the day before, from one of the radiologists, and to be honest, it is my normal quirk to reject new ideas when they disrupt the norm. I like things to stay the way they are most of the time, even when change may be an improvement. But listening to Becky talk, it dawned on me, change was going to happen one way or the other, so I'd better pick an option Shelly could live with.

The J/G tube would be inserted into the same opening as her G-tube, but radiology would have to thread it into her intestine, by-passing the stomach for the *Jejunal* part to be set properly. There would be a tube coming out with separate access for the stomach and the intestines.

Presumably, I could send her to school with bolus feeds to go into her stomach, and later hook her to the machine for a dripping, continuous feed. She could still have some freedom.

As I write this, I know life didn't continue as easily as I imagined or hoped. I am again grateful for the way God allowed things about our future to unveil gently to me. I do have a slow brain for change.

Earlier, I had again impatiently changed my flight home, this time to that very night- irrational, but I wanted to see Isaiah on his sixteenth birthday. I'd not be getting there until midnight, but reasoned at least I'd get to hear a music evaluation for piano he was having the next day.

Two things reverted the flight plan back to Saturday. First, there was a security breach at the Atlanta Airport, causing an evacuation and rerouting of planes. Since 9/11 all airport security was, of course, taken seriously.

Secondly, Shelly was going to get her J/G-tube that evening.

Our small world shifts.

So, after all, it was on Saturday when we came home. Nurses were smiling through tears as we left the floor. Rose, with Betsy at her side, insisted on pushing Shell's wheelchair down to the cab.

I sat in the back seat and cried, watching out the window, the hospital receding, and wondering if this was the last time we would be making this trip. The threat of diarrhea and dehydration was very real, and finally quite un-fixable.

Things at home turned out better than we had reason to hope. Shell never does what we expect her to do, and the awful diarrhea we dealt with, both at home and at school, soon gave way to constipation. Constipation has its own issues, but we can deal with it, and Shell gladly went back to school, being fed small amounts in her G-tube during the day.

Becca gave us respite for four days while we took a fast run up to Pennsylvania for my parent's fiftieth anniversary. We magnanimously brought home the flu from our trip, and we soon found out Shell could weather even a major illness while coping with a new feeding method, so things assumed a sort of normalness in our lives.

It could surely never last.

## ~ Twenty~Nine ~

*L*et's try to be normal. Let's give school another shot and *everyone*, please try to be normal.

A note from Shell's Orientation and Mobility specialist included the following:

"Shelly's continued use of the cane jeopardizes the safety of those working with her and those passing by her."

Answering the age-old question of whether or not blind-canes mix with blind rage.

I woke on a Tuesday morning, mid-way through February, thinking it would be just another day in paradise. While flushing Shell's J/G-tube, I saw it had blown a hole and tried to stop the leak by putting in one of her G-tubes to substitute, a cork of sorts.

I quickly called Becky Hoagland and she conferred with the GI doctors, everyone deciding it would be better if we flew up there to be checked out.

So the Chaos Theory brings on the Chaos of Preparation. I called Becca, catching her before the bus left, to let her know Shell would be gone - called the airline and got a flight for one-thirty p.m. Called Tom, who was at work, and told him I was once again heading to Ohio. Called Social Services and told them, too. Called Columbus Don and let him know we were going to be in his neck of the woods.

Crossing my fingers in hopes I'd not missed making any important calls; I turned my attention to packing.

I packed Shell's clothes for an undetermined amount of time, and packed my clothes likewise. I packed meds for Shell and toiletries for me. I packed toys for Shell's pleasure, a Bible, a poem book and a journal for my sanity.

Crossing my fingers I'd not missed packing anything important, I turned my attention to chores.

I watered all the plants, fed the dogs, cats and

birds. I swept the floors, cleaned up Shell's room, washed the dishes, did two loads of laundry, took a shower, gave Shell a bath and shampoo, wrote out instructions for house duties, and wrote out instructions for Isaiah's homeschool lessons. Whew!

Crossing my fingers I'd not missed doing any major chores, I turned my attention to leaving. I hugged Isaiah and had prayer with him, hugged the dogs and promised I'd be home soon, hugged Tom at Station 2, and had prayer with him.

Crossing my fingers I'd not left anyone feeling unloved, I drove to the airport, grateful for the hour long drive so I could get my crying over with before facing the rest of the day.

And a long day it was. I drove on a full charge of adrenaline and we got to the airport in plenty of time. We put Shell's backpack through the scanner and they searched it thoroughly—I had a bag of change in it, making it look suspicious.

This was before the *Shoe Bomber* but they were about to check my shoes anyway, when the woman at the gate remembered Shell and me from years of flying, and let us pass through. Shell always made an impression, and many airport personnel asked about her when I flew alone.

The first flight went smoothly, but Shell wore out fast. She dehydrated quickly with all the activity and grew angry. Most likely she suffered from a headache and couldn't express the pain in any other way. She lashed out and threw herself around, bruising both herself and me pretty thoroughly.

Columbus Don was waiting for us when the second flight landed. I rejoiced to see him as thoughts of getting Shell into a cab right then were daunting.

We got to the emergency room by four-thirty p.m. and it was a long wait with an unhappy child. Finally, about eight o'clock we got into radiology for a new J/G-tube, and then up to a room before one o'clock in the morning. The room looked so inviting, and Columbus Don had ordered Pizza, which soon arrived. I could remember heating up a bit of rice for an odd early morning breakfast, but hadn't eaten all day. I was famished. After we ate, Don left and I crashed about three o'clock in the morning, thanking God for the safe travels.

Ridiculously early the next morning, I woke, worried about missing the doctor's rounds. Fueled by strong coffee from downstairs, I tried to keep my plans flexible for the possibilities the day may bring, and we soon found out Shell was being released.

A former nurse of hers named Bonnie, came upstairs for a visit as we got packed up to go, and we got pictures and hugs all around. Then Columbus Don, (dear, sweet man), showed up to take us to the airport for our early afternoon flight.

At this point, the Chaos Theory determined the flight would have a short delay, and then a definite cancellation due to a thunderstorm in Cincinnati.

Anyone who has experienced a delayed flight while caring for a child knows it is a comparative luxury to be delayed alone. In both cases, arriving late to a destination is problematic, but waiting with children is a bit of a nightmare involving maintaining tenuous sanity for the sake of appearances.

Are there too few diapers, not enough bottles, and far less patience than you had packed in your carry-on? Any outside chance you will have a happy baby or quiet toddler is none. Nada. Nein. Disgruntled adult fliers quickly stop viewing your child as a cutie, and now seem prepared to step in and give you lengthy lessons in discipline. Such is the mortification icing on your misery cake.

A kind airport official from our customary Delta airlines must have taken pity on us, seeing how hard it was to keep Shell amused, and then quieted, and then from exploding altogether. He arranged to get us on a 4:20 flight to Lexington just as the thunderstorms hit the airport there in Columbus.

It felt like we'd never be airborne as we sat in the plane for another hour and a half waiting for the worst of it to pass over. A thoughtful man across the aisle from us let me use his cell phone to leave a message for Tom.

For whatever reason Shell has for whatever it is she does, she was quite content to sit out the time on the airplane. She happily drummed her fingers on the tray table, pulled the shade up and down, lightly rocked herself and made the kind of noises I know to mean she's glad to be right where she is. When we finally headed down the runway, she gleefully shivered in anticipation of take-off and spent the rest of the flight laughing with her hands waving in the air, while the turbulence sent the rest of the passengers into quiet prayer mode. Ah, my child... she loves a rocky ride.

## ~ *Thirty* ~

*F*or a while things went on in their usual shaky way. Shell developed a virus a couple of days after the hospital stay, and ran fevers over 103°, keeping her home from school for many days. She had lost some weight and slept for long periods of time, or more often, had long days with almost no sleep at all.

By the end of February, we were getting calls from the nurse at Shell's school, worried Shelly had "body fluids". In other words, her feeding tube would leak around the site.

From home, I found it hard to judge how critical this information might seem to others. I was used to so much fluid. 'Some' on a chair at school - most obviously her feeds - didn't strike my panic button.

*So? Wipe it off and get over it. The kid leaks. She's broken. What can I say?* I badly wanted to say.

Okay, I know I sound flippant, but I was really, really tired. On lucky nights, we got between four and five hours of actual sleep - but *never* at once.

In addition to Shell's insomnia, there was a rash of fires keeping Tom on the go. Late into the wee hours I tried to do things like needlepoint a wedding gift, read books and keep a journal. These things kept me up because I couldn't do them during regular office hours.

Those daylight hours were crammed with driving to and from violin lessons, piano lessons, Toastmaster meetings, homeschool meetings, writing up our homeschool newsletter, the usual desperation housework, laundry and meals. There were supplies to order and keep tabs on, and phone calls to and from every single living human being on the planet. There were plans going on for our son's August wedding and I was helping Isaiah prepare for piano camp in the summer and college in the fall. In the meantime, my family up north seemed to be falling apart at the seams and I couldn't be there to help them with anything.

You know what I mean... usual life.

As it turned out, we spent a lot of time flying back and forth right up until spring. I hoped to put off the longer hospital stay, expected when Shell was to get a separate J-tube. Involving surgery, a tube similar to the G-tube would be implanted, but in the upper section of the small intestine, the *Jejunum*, below the stomach.

## ~ Thirty One ~

*C*all a cab.

I'm not a city girl. Cabs are not second-nature to me. I've grown accustomed to locating them at the airports, but I'd feel foolish flagging one down on the street. Most likely, I'd begin by apologizing for bothering the cabbie, and ask if it would be okay if I got a ride - if it wouldn't take him out of his way. Then I'd probably get flustered and forget where I wanted to go. I think it's a learned skill.

The taxi drivers Shelly and I rode with were as diverse as one would expect in a city the size of Columbus, Ohio—many nationalities and accents, a neighborhood retiree, a student working through college.

When I first started going to Children's by cab, I didn't know if I should chat with the driver, or shut up and let the man concentrate. And what topics besides the weather would be appropriate? I'm sure the cabbies taking me in those days never thought twice about the dilemma this posed for me, the uninitiated.

Then there is the matter of the meter. How could I not watch it like a hawk? The less money I had on me, the faster it seemed to add up. And numbers just fly out of my head, so if I get into the cab knowing what is in my wallet, I soon forget because the meter has my mind fluttering.

I check and re-check, trying to imagine (without using any actual math skills) what I should give as a tip. All of this being balanced, again, by the denominations I had on me. Do I expect him to have change for a fifty dollar bill? The answer to *that* one is *"No!"* and much time wasted when we arrive at the airport as he protests and reluctantly helps me find change. (Even with my poor math skills, I'm guessing change from a fifty is too much of a tip for a seventeen dollar fare.)

Sometimes I'd get a grump, or a smokey cab, or what I discerned to be a much longer route and bigger charge, with "road construction" being the culprit. I'd try not to annoy the grump, crack a window for the smoke, and not tip much if we went through Canada to get to the hospital.

I was winging it on etiquette.

But very often I found warm and caring souls driving those cabs - The man whose daughter's life was saved at Children's Hospital, and he speaks of the place with reverence - the man saving his money to bring his family to the States from Nigeria, and kept checking with me to see if "your little girl is *okay?*"

One day we flew in for a quick J/G replacement. Tom had been lifting Shell into her bed the night before and the tube got caught on the bed rails and pulled out. He felt terrible, but things happen.

I flew to Columbus with her in the morning, and everything went so well I was crossing my fingers to get home by nightfall, J/G intact and make it to Isaiah's piano recital the next day, no big deal.

The replacement went smoothly and the radiologist joked, suggesting I tell Tom he had added an extra two cc's to the bubble keeping it in place, just for him.

I called a cab and went outside with Shell to wait in the warm April sun. We waited and waited and the cab never came. We walked along the sidewalk, smelling the hyacinth and sat on the concrete wall listening to a nearby pregnant teenager rant about her parents. I carried Shell on my back and twirled her to imaginary music.

Finally, afraid of missing our flight, I took her back in and called another cab company, but by this time Shell was in no mood to wait another moment. She was thrashing, hitting, crying out and trying to bite my shoulder when I held her. She was the terrorist who everyone watched as they waited for their own rides.

Finally, the cab pulled in and I struggled to get her settled and belted in as she flung herself all over the back seat. I started to bleed from the scratches she'd inflicted and she made herself black and blue from battling every- thing within reach. I could only imagine what my out-of- control child must have looked like to the cab driver, so I started to explain her situation: being without much fluid or nutrition for about 24-hours and her dehydration.

He adjusted his rear-view mirror so I could see his kind eyes and said, "Don't you worry - there's nothing she can hurt in here we can't fix later." He turned off his me- ter, and when we got to the airport, charged us much less than I know the fare to be.

His understanding was a touch of peace on my soul. We ended up with long delays between flights, but the re- membrance of his kindness kept me calm.

Only one action of well-placed sympathy from a workaday cab driver—the world can change in a moment.

One day we flew with an entire high school baseball team. Seems to me every plane that ever crashed, in the history of aviation, carried a sports team of some sort.

## ~ *Thirty-Two* ~

*S*helly was happy to go to school most days, but not always happy while there. We had a lot of phone calls back and forth; days she would come home early, or hurt too much to go at all. Gas pains would well up fast and she would be lashing out in her distress. We had no crystal ball to see into the future of how she would survive or if she would survive.

So, one day, I decided she should drive a car. Sure, she'd never go off to college, get married or have kids, but there should be at least one 'rite-of-passage' she could participate in.

I built up the mood by signing to her—*SHE was going to drive!* I clapped with her and we danced around so she would know a 'big deal' thing was coming up!

She marched importantly up to our jeep as if she knew—ah, I love that look. There were a few moments of confusion as I directed her to the driver's seat and had her sit on my lap, but I kept signing excitedly to her, and she took the wheel like a pro. I guided her right hand to the shifter and we put it into reverse.

I could see she was starting to understand the concept of control, harking back to bike riding and the little green tractor she loved when she was younger. Backing up in our yard, I let her flex the wheel exaggeratedly and she started laughing. She laughed and giggled all the way down the driveway to the road, and all the way back up. She laughed even harder as I helped her push on the horn, beeping loud enough for even her to hear. She gasped with big belly laughs, tears in her eyes, by the time we got back to the house, gunning the motor a bit for a final flourish as we pulled into the yard!

Shell was sixteen years old, and she had passed the

deaf/blind driving test with flying colors.

Enough was enough. We decided to place the perma-Nent J-tube. I conferred with Children's Hospital and Dr. King, and sorted my life out at home. (*Okay*, I don't actually sort anything of the sort, but I do what I can.) On the Thursday morning before Derby Day in May of 2002, after almost three hours of sleep the night before, Tom drove us to the airport and left us in time to get to work.

Shell got her preferred seat by the window, and as she checked the edges of everything in reach for weak spots she could pull apart, I distracted myself from thoughts of the upcoming surgery.

I did this by picking the brains of the man to my right. He owned a Long John Silver's franchise in Okla-homa, had a nineteen-year-old daughter, an office at home, and made the merging of his company and several other big name companies' sound interesting. Completely out of my normal line of thought, so perfect conversation for the flight.

Columbus Don picked us up and drove us to the sur-gery center, where they took Shelly in an hour earlier than scheduled. Don and I ate some lunch at the cafeteria, stay-ing distracted with talk, but got back to a long wait any-way. Surgery lasted three hours and both Don and I were able to go into the recovery room as she.

Shell was angry with her oxygen being measured and angry with her bandages. They had found a small vein for the surgery, and Dr. King was hoping it would stay inserted for several days.

Right. This is Shelly-No-Veins we're talking about.

Following surgery we headed up to our room on 4-Tower South, the floor below her 'first home'. I was so tired I couldn't see straight, calling Tom and crashing to sleep by ten p.m.

The next morning began at five o'clock with a sore, restless child. By the time Dr. King came in, two hours later, Shell had torn off the bandages, but things were looking good. We gave her a pain reliever and she relaxed enough to sleep some more.

At eleven o'clock, the vein 'blew', lasting longer than I betted it would. The nurses found another vein in her right arm, under her old pic-line. Her poor sweet body, covered in scars. That line didn't last a full ten minutes. Another attempt was made in her right wrist, and we all tried hard to distract her from her misery. She had to wear a drainage bag attached to her G-tube site for fluid overflow and she was having none of it - ripping the bag off when she could.

Shell got more pain medicine in the evening and I was glad to see her finally fall asleep at night. How can you get so much more tired sitting around in a hospital than if you worked at a job all day?

The IV line on Shelly's wrist lasted well into the next day. Midway through the afternoon, she made it her mission in life to pull it out. Her nurse Betsy and I made it our mission in life to keep it intact. Shell fought like a banshee, swinging her free arm around to smack anyone in her reach. Columbus Don came in for a visit and when she felt who it was, she threw her arms around his neck like he was her personal savior. She let him rock her for a long time, sniffling, but in a couple hours again fought so hard we had to put her into the bed. As we discussed her situation, she slyly put her hands behind her back and worked the IV out.

Stubborn Redhead.

No other lines would work - everything blew right away. Finally it was agreed she should get increased J-tube amounts and see how she did. My last thought before sleeping was, 'poor Nurse Betsy!'

The next day we dealt with Shell's anger again. She must have had a headache, and she even pulled clumps of her hair out in frustration. I could add those to the ones I was pulling out of my own hair. It is hard to see your child hurting and not know where - or how to make it better.

I learned how to extract her stomach fluids from a drainage bag attached to the G-tube site and measure them. Brave Betsy was back with us for the third straight day. Other nurses from Shell's past would come by to visit her as the hours stretched on. I went to bed by eleven o'clock, hoping to catch up on sleep, but Shell was angry.

I can handle her anger better than her tears. She cries so rarely it breaks my heart. Still, we had another awful night.

For some reason her pain medicine came in pill form the next morning. Too tired and frustrated to deal with the wait for a liquid form, I quietly crushed a pill, added water and gave to her via G-tube. She spent the day in the rise and fall of crankiness but things finally calmed down toward evening. I had home to look forward to tomorrow.

Shell was released by the doctors with orders to keep the stitches in for 10 days. It would be six to seven weeks before she could get a 'button' J-tube that I would be able to replace by myself at home.

Tom drove the four hours to Columbus and we made a bed in the back seat for Shell and took her home by car. Even imagining a plane trip home after this surgery was too overwhelming.

Home, Sweet Home—
God bless us, one and all!

Shelly bounced in and out of school for the rest of the year, which ended later in May than usual. We often flew back to Columbus for a fix-up, or went to the nearest city's hospital for repairs which they couldn't do, and so eventually flew to Columbus anyway.

It was an incredibly stressful time, made all the more so by Shell's increasing anger. Some of it I could attribute to pain, but some of it seemed to be coming from anything and everything else.

I was constantly black and blue along my legs and arms, as I took the worst of what she could dish out, keeping between her and hard places so she'd not hurt herself even worse.

She was black and blue also, and I reasoned if I had to take her in to an emergency room, where the doctors didn't know her; they would assume I'd beaten my child, this child I held in my arms with only love. I figured I'd go to jail for the rest of my life and forfeit my good name. Ah yes, but maybe I could also get some sleep there.

~ *Thirty-Three* ~

*O*ur worst episode came in June, during a trip to Columbus to finally exchange her long J-tube with a 'Button' one I could replace at home.

As usual, I was up most of the night before the flight, worried I would forget something or at least forget to do something. My nerves felt like they were traveling on top of my skin so about two a.m. I took a long, hot bath. I felt better but still could only sleep in snatches, and was dismayed to see how soon the 4:45 alarm sounded. I had coffee with Tom and then had to rush Shell through her dressing to get out of the house before 6 o'clock.

At the airport, I easily found parking and Shell walked for several yards before turning to me to be carried. She was already tired so I hoisted her eighty-five pounds onto my back and ran for the terminal, my heavy backpack flapping around at my side. Sensing Shelly's shirt was already soaked from her leaking J-tube site, I raced her into a bathroom for a quick change.

Our first flight, which I would later look back on fondly, went just fine. At the Cincinnati airport I carried Shell all over the place while waiting, afraid to let her ride in a wheelchair because she was so bent on destroying them.

Arriving in Columbus, Don met the plane and drove us right to the Outpatient Care Center, where I struggled to hold The Bean while filling out papers and signing everything put in front of me without a moment to read it.

Dr. King's nurse, Jackie, measured both the G-tube and the J-tube to order the correct sizes. There was a long delay finding the right ones and I started to get nervous about the one-thirty flight, thinking I should have tried for a later one. When the new 'button' J and G tubes were in place, it looked like Shell would be much more comfortable from then on.

Long past noon we finally raced to the airport, hoping to somehow still make it, only to find a long line looping around poles of roped off sections. Happily, they were calling out to passengers scheduled on the one-thirty flight and took us ahead of the crowd. We said good-bye to Don at the X-Ray machine, and I kept looking back to see him waving as we rounded the corner.

That's when the real nightmare began. Shell had been getting cranky, but we zoomed along too fast to let it be a problem. Now she was furious. She knew where we were, and knew it usually involved some sort of waiting, which she was in no mood for.

I carried her on my back, abandoning our bags like terrorists. I took her into the handicapped stall in the bathroom for another shirt change, and she angrily beat on me and the stall - trying to bite, scratching like a panther and crying her wild scream. I kept her there because it wouldn't be any better going out, hoping she would tire, but at one point as she flailed against the stall door, it opened.

Standing at the sink was a woman janitor. Her look indicated she was certain I was abusing the child beyond belief, and it appeared she was 'this close' to calling the authorities. She glared at me in disgust and muttered something under her breath, which made me blush to my toes in horror of what we must look like.

I couldn't stop to explain to her that the blood was my own, and Shelly was the unlikely abuser. I would have been just as indignant if I saw someone else in my position, and I vowed then and there to give the benefit of mercy in every situation I ran into from then on.

I carried my bundle of joy back to the waiting area only to find the plane now delayed until almost two thirty.

I found a more or less quiet spot and Shell proceeded to make it less so. There was no limit to her fury and she fought with every fiber of her being as I tried to keep her arms and legs circled in mine and safe.

By this time my heart was completely calm. I did what I could do and realized it was one of those moments in life when there is nothing else to be done but what was being done. There was no one to help, no magic emergency number to make things better, no backing out or backing down. There was only this—an angry child and the Mama who loved her more than life.

So there we were... and here is the marvel and the wonderment I have thought of ever since. We were surrounded by businessmen. And every single one of those suited, coiffed, pressed and composed men were like grace from God Himself. Not one of them left in a huff, not one of them stared at us in dismay; not one of them spoke an angry word or worse yet for me, a kind one. Kindness can undo me completely.

To a man, they ignored our presence, and formed a barrier for us from the rest of the waiting area. They will never know how much I needed them to do just what they did that day. It's not as if they were unaware of us. That would have been impossible in any case. But they acted unaware of us, an act almost holy in its nature. I hummed a tune to my angry deaf child - an Irish lullaby - and kept the peace I felt somewhere in the eye of Shelly's tornado.

Finally allowed to board, we found ourselves entering an oven-like heat on the plane, and discovered the delay had been due to a faulty air conditioner.

Let me just mention something here: being hot does not improve Shelly's mood one whit. She began to dismantle the plane's interior and before I could stop her she actually peeled a strip under the window from alongside her seat and threw it behind her, whacking a man two seats back.

I began to pray - not for a safe flight - I was well be-yound such frivolity. I was quite willing to go into a spiral-ing, nose-dive plane crash at this point. No, I only prayed, in lieu of such an easy way out, for Shell to be calmed, somehow.

Arriving in Cincinnati I was not at all surprised to find our delay had caused us to miss the connecting flight to Lexington. Juggling a squirming and unhappy Shell with our carry-ons, I negotiated at the desk for the next possibil-ity at three forty-five.

It didn't show up.

Word got around—we may get lucky at four o'clock.

Shell passed out from exhaustion, her head heavy on my shoulder. I wanted to pass out too, but just sat still, grateful for the lull.

At twenty after four, a woman from the airline who had been concerned about us and had promised to let us know as soon as she herself knew anything, came over and told us we could board now. Shell, as I rose and gathered up the backpack, was upset at the disturbance. We got as far as the door of the plane when an official stopped us to say they didn't have a flight crew.

*Not a problem*, I thought. *I'll serve the blasted drinks myself!*

The wheelchair we secured was soon stripped of its non-essentials - like sides. I whirled Shell in and out of the rows of seats in the waiting area and when she tired of whirling, I signed to her we'd soon 'fly'! This seemed to be a boldfaced signing lie, as the new word around the waiting area: there was no pilot.

*Not a problem*, I thought, *I'll fly the blasted thing myself!*

Eternity surely passes faster than our time that night in the waiting area. Perhaps in order to pass the buck somehow, the nice airline woman came for us once again and had us board the plane, by ourselves. Finally, other passengers were allowed to board and finally, much later, the pilot himself also boarded. So we headed home.

Of course, a thunderstorm struck Lexington as we arrived, causing us to circle and circle and circle - it couldn't have been any other way. Perfect ending as it turned out - our very last trip to Columbus...

End of an era.

## ~ *Thirty-Four* ~

*"It is such a secret place, the land of tears."*
*(Le Petit Prince)*

*N*ow I entered a part of my life - pulling me into a small world - leaving the other behind me. It didn't happen overnight, but I felt it almost daily.

Shell stayed home for the summer, which was a natural enough time to be home. We had not been able to arrange for an intervenor to work with her, as we had hoped, but there were so many 'bad' days no one would have lasted anyway.

The anger grew worse than ever and Shelly would lash out in new and innovative ways, making it necessary to watch her constantly. I had taken to trimming the little sides of her pull-ups as she would feel for them with her sensitive fingers, and finding the slightest irregularity, would rip them apart and throw them off the bed in shreds. Lately she left off the examination and assuming the faults existed, ripping through the side panels as soon as she was changed. I could have replaced them a thousand times a day, but instead I told her she'd have to wear it like that, and left her with the chic 'loin-cloth look'.

The 'Furies' came to a head about mid-July. I averaged around 3-4 hours of sleep in snatches every night, so tired that I constantly fantasized about going to a quiet motel and collapsing on the bed, hoping not to move or be found until weeks later, by 'the authorities'.

I cried often from stress and fatigue. My family 'up North' was being demolished by a drama, keeping me on the phone constantly, trying to patch holes in a cheese-cloth-dike of relationships.

One son was preparing for a big wedding, need I say

more? The other son was slipping off into adulthood with all the normal theater involved - (may God bless him with a teenager one day). Our eldest daughter was straining to see how far her desire for more independence would get her, and we were straining to keep her in-check with reality.

I had many violin students in and out, who often skipped lessons without notice. Tom was getting frustrated with our inability to go anywhere together, as one of us always needed to be home with Shelly. He wasn't saying anything about it, but he could see this was yet another year I'd not be accompanying him to Family Camp. I wasn't saying anything about it, but was wondering if I'd be able to even go to our son's wedding in Ohio.

I thought of my prayer life as pretty active, keeping God up to date on everything He already knew, but at this point, I didn't even know what to pray about. So many things were out of my control, swirling me into a vortex.

Praying about Shelly, having been through so much with her, (and having no idea I had only touched the surface of where we would end up), my prayers seemed confusing, even to me. (Thank you, Lord, for letting us know you understand, even when we don't have the words!)

"What do I do, Lord? I am at the end, and she is not. I don't know how to make life better for her, and she is miserable."

The day came when everything seemed to fall apart at once. Shell had been up most of the night, impatiently throwing away every 'toy' I handed her. I dragged myself all over the place retrieving a new object for her to play with. I was exhausted when Tom left for work in the morning, and just wanted to lie in on my mattress surrounded by dogs and have my bible time in peace. Instead I found myself with a few unexpected teenager problems, more frustrating extended-family feuding, and a horrific headache.

Michelle had finally fallen asleep, but we in a temper and pulled apart her button J-tube. She went ballistic when I had to replace it, fighting like a wild animal caught in a trap. Her shirt drenched with awful smelling stomach fluid, but when I tried to change it, she belted me, whacking my eye socket which started swelling immediately. I perversely hoped for a black-and-blue shiner to warrant the exceptional pain and flashing stars.

As my poor, possessed redhead grabbed for my arms, which she raked her nails into, drawing blood, I grabbed for the phone. By this time I had Dr. Murray's number well imbedded in my long term memory, but I had never called him in a circumstance quite like this.

His voice, when he came on, undid me with its concern and I burst into tears. The dear man stayed with me as I fought to even speak, and when I did, it was mostly incoherent, semi-hysterical babbling. He patiently tried to sort out what was going on, even as Shell reached over and bit me hard on the arm, and worse yet, began hitting her own head on the side board of her bed.

I placed myself to cushion her, and she sat up, seeming to settle down somewhat, a hint of Helen Keller - calm before the storm - look on her face. Imagining this was a truce, I foolishly turned my focus to the phone call.

An explosion of water brought my attention back to Shelly, who had reached the bottom of her mattress and ripped out the plug on the waterbed. Water cascaded over the bedsides by the time I located the errant plug across the room and replaced it. I lifted Shelly's wet self from the bed onto my lap in the rocking chair and wrapped my arms around her, both of us crying and hugging. We were such a mess.

That phone call, however, brought about a much needed change in our lives. Dr. Murray asked if we would consider the possibility Shelly may be experiencing a chemical depression and had no other way to express her angst.

It was as if a reasonable, sensible answer existed right there, waiting for someone to call it into the light.

In the meantime, he promised to confer with Dr. Fulkerson and order a sedative. Momentarily confused, I wondered if he would write the prescription for Shelly or for me...

So, we ended the summer in a shaky state, and with Isaiah heading off to college, Shell would return once more to the middle school. They were the same age, but at sixteen, on far different paths.

I had protested at IEP meetings any notion of her entering the new world of High School. I could think of nothing more pointless. She may have been the right age for it in years, but she was still smaller than most kids at the middle school. Life was complex enough without more changes. Not to mention the fact she had so far failed to grasp even the basic concepts of 1492 or long division. We were given one more year—a grace period. Period.

## ~ *Thirty-Five* ~

*S*helly needed to be fed on a round-the-clock basis, through her J-tube alone; so we got a portable pack, allowing everything to be handled at school, trailing a bit of tubing about. It was either this or nothing, and my mind couldn't wrap around the notion of Shell being attached to her bed for the rest of her life.

As if she had gone every day-
As if she had expected me to say
This very thing-
As if it was all a part of her plans-

"You are going to school," I signed to Shelly, and she left in high expectation, head high, floppy hat in place, jaunty step, tubes and drainage bag safe in her fanny pack - energetic for the moment.

I agreed to do her transportation this year to and from school. When we arrived on her first day Becca came out to meet us at the very moment Shell balked at whole process. It took some convincing, but we managed to persuade her to go in. I don't know if she rebelled at not getting to take the bus or my handing her off at school instead of at home. Shell didn't like things to change. She liked routine, and it took an effort to alter this girl's way of thinking.

I was relieved to now have a few hours a day to finish preparing plans to go to the wedding. Becca had agreed to do respite for us and we were going to be gone for two nights, God willing.

Shell lasted two days in school before needing to come home early, the start of a trend. Even when she lasted all day, she would be exhausted upon getting home.

I could see how much it was taking out of her to let her life be normal.

Our 'time out' for the wedding went by fast, and we were gradually finding more and more of our days being spent holding Shelly, or pushing her on the swing when the weather allowed. My legs worried me by aching from the lack of circulation. I imagined blood clots of the kind you'd get in an airplane - but in the airplane you'd not be holding eighty-five pounds of child. The worse Shell felt, the closer she cuddled and some days I found myself having to put her in bed just to walk around for relief. She would, of course, climb right out and stretch her line to the limit, clearing the room of anything in her reach.

As often as he could, Tom would 'spell' me, so I could practice my violin or do some mowing, which I loved. On the Wednesdays he didn't work, or could trade a few hours, he would hold her so I could get to gymnastics where I could ease both my body and mind.

What I resented though, was Shell's imperative in-sistence I not hold a book and hold her at the same time. I had all the time in the world to read, but she would have none of it. When I put my foot down about it, she flew into a rage inevitably ending with some part of her tubing being destroyed. On this she was adamant: I must always let her believe she had my undivided attention. I should have been paid for doing movie reviews, as many as we ended up watching over those years.

I compromised by placing poem book beside the ball, or the chair, and memorized poetry for hours. I often put on music videos and danced with Shell around the room un-til we were both exhausted and laughing. Tom attached a swing to the ceiling and, being careful not to tangle her feeding tube, we pushed her until she tired. And tire she did, more and more easily, and for longer and longer peri-ods.

Things were not going so well at school, not for Shelly, not for her teachers. Shell didn't feel well, even when she felt her best, and daily got angrier at her new tube, being hooked up, and with boredom - it doesn't matter how big you dot it in Braille, the word 'Saturday' and other similar words, just don't make sense to someone like the Bean, who measures days in a far different manner than the rest of the world.

What began as occasional early pick-up days, turned into more frequent calls to home and I found myself making two and sometimes three trips to school every day to replace her J-tube. She took the place apart and once, even broke someone's glasses, lashing out. How do you say you don't feel good and are terribly unhappy?

The end came in mid-September - having lasted only twenty-one actual school days, Shelly got kicked out of school for good.

I was too upset to be rational about it. The explanation was delivered by the school nurse, who had earlier admonished me about Shelly's leaking site.

"I hate to be the bearer of bad news," she said, "but they wouldn't let Shell back in because she had an open wound."

"Open wound, indeed," I fumed. "It's a surgically placed port for a feeding tube!"

All the way home with my 'problem child' in tow, I alternated between rants and tears. If they had said she was getting the boot for being unmanageable, or too angry to be in a classroom, I could at least respect the motion, empathize with it - agree with it even. But this...

This was sliding her out the back door.

A month after Shell was expelled from school for her 'open wound,' I returned when they asked me to attend a meeting to address "concerns."

"Claire, tell us of your concerns."

"I don't have any concerns."

"But you must have some concerns."

"If Shelly can work for a while with Becca during the day, it would be fine. If that isn't possible, then I have no concerns."

Nurse Bouncer was there, but I didn't address my concerns about the ability to discern an open wound from a surgically placed hole. As for fluids, I assumed any child who drooled in the special needs classroom got the boot too - surely Shell wasn't singled out.

An assistant in charge of irony said I needed to write an 'excuse' note for Shelly's twelve days off from school.

To the amusement of her dear teachers, I said, "No way. You people kicked her out. Why should I write the excuse? I don't excuse her. I think she's pretty inexcusable at this point."

Besides—I think they just like reading my notes.

# ~ Thirty-Six ~

Thus, ended Shell's life as a student. We tried having Becca work at home with her, but it was so contrary to Shell's idea of 'normal' she'd have nothing to do with it - even when we set everything up, classroom style. Shell was angry and once again I was home alone with her, but now it was for good.

So, it was my time to learn some things. I began to learn about what I really needed, as opposed to what I thought 'my time' should be all about.

Seeing this was the end of the rope for 'me' time, I felt pretty sorry for myself some days. I we up exhausted every morning, in a state of deep depression, shell shocked and knowing I could be doing this same thing over and over again for years. I would get coffee, feed and change Shell, be holding her by eleven o'clock in the morning - and hold her all day long.

I began to fear God had forgotten me, and I could hardly blame him. I reasoned I'd finally gotten so insignificant and small I must have disappeared from His radar. I cried often in despair.

When the pain in my legs became constant, I battled with social services and got them to purchase a recliner so I could hold Shelly with my legs up some of the time. I worried about a blood clot, as Shell would dig in as close to me as she could, tucking her feet under her and cutting off the circulation in my legs.

I had no one to turn to but my already overwhelmed Tom, facing his new life of being the one who did the other stuff. He did all the grocery shopping, and the cooking. He took Shell as often as possible, and let me have time to mow the yard or take a break.

The days were dark and long in my mind, and I

thought they would remain so for good. By the middle of November, almost a year after losing her IV lines, Shell seemed to worsen and grow weaker. Her hair thinned and it seemed such an effort to even hold her head up. I contacted Columbus Hospital and Dr. Murray ordered blood work... it showed very low electrolytes. The remedy, it appeared, was to recycle her stomach fluids through her J-tube—yum!

It took a while to get comfortable with the whole idea. Sometimes the fluids were green or blue or yellow, which always tinted the formula going by machine to her gut. Nurses do this all the time in the hospitals, I guess, but I bet it wasn't their favorite job.

Shelly revived drastically with the change and it became an easy enough habit, measuring and re-using...

So, where we live the rules are pretty strict. "You eat your breakfast, or you'll get it for lunch, young lady!"

## ~ *Thirty-Seven* ~

I'm trying to justify my existence.
I feel I should be doing something
Big and important –
And I'm not.
I should be writing a book, painting a masterpiece,
re-doing a room, learning how to spin and weave. I should
be getting a degree on-line,
Becoming a potter, cutting out coupons,
Fostering more children.
Or what?
What should I be doing besides wrapping mylife
around the life of this child?
I'm tired all the time-
I'll do those things someday-
Someday.
Someday when my life changes.


*~ Lamentations 3 ~*
*I am the man who has seen affliction by the rod of*
*his wrath. He has driven me away and made me walk in*
*darkness rather than light; indeed, he has turned his hand*
*against me again and again, all day long.*
~ * ~

$\mathcal{I}$wake in tears, facing the dim light of the western window from my mattress on the floor. My soul is bereft. I rock my lost self in a misery too deep to express, even to myself. I am alone in this world with Shelly. There is no one - and God had deserted me. I cannot hear His answers to my prayers. I cannot feel His comfort in my heart. I am alone. I am alone. The days are silent. I don't welcome the sounds of the world I'm no longer a part of.

I leave the radio and television off. I don't want

the news. I don't want to hear what is being sold and bought, and I don't care if it rains or snows. I am alone – alone – alone. One quiet minute to the next.

I am grateful Shell doesn't speak; she has no words I must listen to; she has no questions when I have no answers. I am grateful the dogs follow me anyway. When I am mute they follow me still, from room to room. I reach for them and bury my tears in their coats, patient looks in steady quiet eyes - no recriminations for my silence.

~ * ~

*I remember my affliction and my wandering, the bitterness and the gall. I well remember them, and my soul is downcast within me.*

~ * ~

"Why?" I ask my God. Why have you left me? Am I too small? Did you forget me because my life is too small? Was I a momentary thought in your mind, but forgotten when the door shut behind me?

I am a scrap of paper in the corner- a dead branch in the woods- a whimper lost to the wind.

My life is too meaningless to count.

I am invisible.

I hold my child and we rock by the hour, my pleas to be saved from this unheard and unanswered. My face is like one unrecognizable.

I beg to be heard, but hear no response. I beg to be remembered but feel imperceptible. I am lost--I am drowning—I am alone.

I search the scriptures for a message to revive me, to bring me what I want. I forget I don't know what it is I want.

I would not be separated from this child for the world, but I have given up my life to care for her. I think I am asking for relief, for respite by God's own hand, as I'd trust no other with her.

~ * ~

151

*He has walled me in so I cannot escape; he has weighed me down with chains. Even when I call out or cry for help, he shuts out my prayer.*

~ * ~

I have found only dust—my face is to the ground—my throat is closed with words I don't have. There are no ears to understand my pain—I am too alone to be seen, too alone to stay alive—I will for my days to end.

Life seems too interminable and I can only see it stretching one day out to the next, every morning with the same dim window, with the same dim soul—with the void that comes from being abandoned—by the world and by my God. I am alone.

The word I search for is not a response to me - I cannot hear it. I cannot yet hear it.

~ * ~

*Yet this I call to mind and therefore I have hope: Because of the Lord's great love we are not consumed, for his compassions never fail.*

~ * ~

I am in despair far beyond where I have ever gone before. Minutes are days and weeks are months... Until I finally hear one small thing.

"Be Still."

"Be Still." Is all I hear at first.

Be Still. Not a voice from a dream, or a vision from beyond. A command from His word.

Be Still. It is all I can hear and it is all I can do. I am in a place where there is nothing else.

Be Still.

And so I was still, and I waited. Still in my soul as the days went by, quiet and alone. Still in my mind as I held my Shelly.

I was left with the labor of caring for this child's life and I let my heart be still and did what was there for me to do - putting aside what I thought I needed to be happy. No other doors had opened, no miracles had happened, no respite for body or mind. Just do what was mine to do, and Be Still.

Finally, there was a sigh in me. I was still.

I had railed against becoming so small, against fading from the world. I had screamed alone in my cell and searched the darkness for doors and windows of escape and had found none. I had felt the panic and thought it was God leaving me.

I had thought it was my God—leaving me.

My hands stopped their frantic searching. My legs tired of trying to run. My eyes adjusted to the change of light. Then I was ready to hear the rest-

"Be still, and know that I am God."
And I knew.

When He saw I could hear again, He told me what he said to his other friends- 'Oh, you of little faith—why are you afraid?'

The men in the boat in a storm—me in my room in a storm. His rebuke reassured me.

~ * ~

*They are new every morning; great is your faithfulness.*

~ * ~

And so I woke every day to that same western window but now the light from it was a gift and my heart sang to God even before my eyes opened.

"What is man, that Thou art mindful of him? The son of man that thou doest care for him?"

My tears-no longer of despair.

Never again, not for a fleeting moment, will I imagine my God has abandoned me. Sadness may be mine, loneliness and hurt, fear and failure.

But my God does not abandon me.

~ * ~

*I say to myself, "The Lord is my portion: therefore I will wait for him."*

~ * ~

When I came to myself - brushing daily against the angel wings protecting my child - I saw God had never moved at all. He was hidden only by my own panic and fear. He was not silent, as I had supposed - but waited quietly for me to hear Him. He was right there. I led a blessed life because I have been so loved by God.

~ * ~

*The Lord is good to those whose hope is in him, to the one who seeks him;*

*It is good to wait quietly for the salvation of the Lord.*

*For men are not cast off by the Lord forever.*

## ~ Thirty Eight ~

What has changed in my life because of having you in it, Principessa? It is watching every brave day you make your own.

How can I not be brave, after seeing you so fearless? How can I not dare do the things I can see, when you dare while you can't?

I hold you in my arms and you fearlessly fling your body backwards, your hair brushing the ground. You laugh as I pull you back and you fly down again, over and over.

For the joy of it-
For the joy of it you pirouette upside-down from the tire swing, twirling like a ballerina or an ice skater, never dizzy, unafraid.
For the joy of it you stand at the end of your bed and fall straight back, climbing up to fall again, over and over.
For the joy of it you let yourself bounce up in the air from the trampoline, signing "More! More!"
For the joy of it you laugh on roller coasters and the dizzying rides at the park.
For the joy of it you hurl your way down slides, not knowing what's at the bottom.
For the joy of it.

How can I not live my life for the joy of it after knowing you?

I jump from an airplane, unafraid and joyful, taking you with me in my heart. I wish you could be here, Principessa—you would love this.

What has changed in my life because of having you in it, Shelly Bean?

It is watching you patiently endure the days before and behind, by living in the very moment you have right then.

How can I not endure, after seeing you so long-suffering? How do I complain for the trials of my life, when yours is so short and hard?

I never lived with a gut that hurt day after day. I never lived without choices of great and small magnitude.

I never lived without the pleasure of food, or art, or literature.

I never lived without easy conversation, small confidences with a friend, shared secrets.

I never lived without methods to convey my pain or my wants...

I never lived a life silent and dark.

But Shelly Bean....

Until I knew how you lived.

I never really lived.


What has changed in my life because of having you in it, Shell-of-mine?

It is knowing you don't know how to die.

How can I not live, when I've known such a child, who doesn't know how to die?

You don't fear the needles from unseen nurses, or scalpels from unseen doctors.

You don't cry in terror of the darkness which is more your lot than ours.

You don't lock the doors, close the drapes, and draw away from sharp teeth.

You don't test the depth of the ocean and height of the waves.

You don't beg the driver to slow down, or dread the germs from hands that guide you.

You don't know how to die. You nick the edges of death so often, I hold my breath in fear for you, but you just draw another one for yourself... a breath... and then another. You live.

One day you will draw your last, surrounded by angels who will breathe into your sweet spirit as they take you home. But you, who did not know how to die, will not be afraid of going home.

So, when that happens, Shell-of-mine, send me help to know how to live without you—without such a mentor in my arms every day. And I will try to forget what I know about dying—and live.

## ~ Thirty-Nine ~

*I'm* on the phone daily with my family from Pennsylvania. The flame of disease and alcohol caught hold its fuel - the fuel of confusion and hurt and misunderstanding, the fuel of anger and guilt and recriminations.

What seemed impossible in our 'normal' upbringing now is a raging inferno and all of us lie awake at night being scorched by its heat. Heroes emerge—are burned and retire. The structure we knew is gone and we can only stare at the ruin in disbelief - heartsick, weary and withdrawing.

Soon there are only embers in the ashes of what we were and individually from time to time we kick at the coals. Rebuild or not? We don't yet know, and it is years before we poke through the mess and salvage what we can from relationships, each according to his or her own ability to forgive and re-love.

This family chaos caused my mother to be living with my brother and his family for a time, and then move in with us. My mother, whose Alzheimer's seemed about in mid stages, had our parent-child roles reversed. I quaked at what I had added to our family's already strained lives, but I didn't want to look back and feel we didn't try. She arrived the first week in January and stayed with us until the end of February.

Our lives could have put sitcoms to shame for their lackluster humor, but somehow it took a long time and a less exhausted state of mind to get any laughs out of us. Suffice it to say, we all were given plenty of opportunity to grow spiritually, should we find the time to do so.

Great is God, who presented me then with one of the sweetest blessings of my adult life. In my search for help with one of hardest challenges of Alzheimer's - the challenge of caregiving, I started doing on-line research.

Late one evening, when I finally had a few quiet moments, I tapped into a site called, "Caregivers of Alzheimer's". It looked relatively new, but I took a chance on it because I was desperate to connect with people who would know what I was talking about, and perhaps have some answers for me. In many ways, that connection changed my life.

No longer did I feel so alone with this disease. I could find someone on the site day and night, and read their posts or write my own.

I began timidly. I had been so invisible for so long I was afraid I would write to them and never hear a response. That seemed too much to bear and so I used the pen-name Annie. I wasn't ready for 'Claire' to be rejected, but this 'Annie' would be up for the challenge. I wouldn't take it personally if Annie faded into cyberspace.

When my Mother went back to Pennsylvania, I wondered if I should leave the group, but they had already taken me into the fold, and they had grown to love my Shelly as well. I was given encouragement in so many areas of my life and it made me bold to try more things. I didn't have to speak aloud, as I was rusty in speaking, but I could be honest and not worry about criticism.

They were down-to-earth people with similar struggles and shared a delightful sense of humor, keeping everyone sane when we often feared for our sanity.

The family I made there is still with me today. Over the years we have shared our lives, our stories, and our hearts. We have been through each other's losses from that awful disease of Alzheimers and even losses of our own members.

Although we hail from all over the states, and several parts of the world, many of us have managed to meet together where we can physically hug the "cyber" family we know so well.

God is good.

*Stone Walls do not a Prison Make, Nor Iron Bars a Cage...*
*(Richard Lovelace)*

For years we were alone while everyone else moved in circles linked to other circles. Mine was a circle around Shelly. We may have been the ones of which was said, 'They're still alive? I've not seen them in so long. I'd forgotten they existed.'

But we had passed the 'just existing' point and lived.

Every second, every minute, every hour and day, week, month and year, while the world went on with its business we were there as unnoticed as a sigh in the wind. We woke to Shelly's rhythms, her happiness or pain or frustration. We spent the hours when small giggles brought smiles, when impatience brought soothing, when joy was made in the smallest possible measures - Our lives like an atom - small, contained, mostly unseen, not easily divided.

The old house we rented on almost a hundred acres of woods and fields had big rooms and a rounded turret in a front corner. We called it 'the Castle' and sometimes, during those years Shell and I were isolated by her illnesses, we were living as if in some sort of enchantment, a spell suspending us from interaction with most of the world. It was not unusual for two weeks to go by without my leaving the property and there were years when I didn't enter a grocery store.

Commercials on TV seemed like alien drivel.

I lost the craving for fast food and couldn't remember when I'd even tasted a French fry. I didn't know what styles were from year to year, only dressing myself for comfort. Shows with women telling other women they, "first needed to take care of themselves, so they would feel good enough to care for the others in their lives," seemed ludicrous. The concept of pampering didn't mean getting my nails done or going to a hairdresser, but instead the luxury of a hot bath in the middle of the night to ease leg cramps.

Where Shell moved, I moved... from room to room, or step by step. I could be teaching violin in the music room and still be judging the urgency of any sound she made.

I grew less and less comfortable with the 'outside world' and things narrowed down to gymnastics on the Wednesdays Tom could be home, church on the Sundays Tom could be home, and brief trips to the library. I knew who would be in those places and was mostly at ease there.

Eventually my speaking skills with those outside the family grew rusty. I would find silences to be normal, even long pauses before answering questions. I formulated thoughts in my mind and measured them out, unsure of their reception.

Most of the time, I felt invisible. Most of the time, I was invisible.

I reserved a time each day for reading my Bibles. Two pages in English - two pages in French. Then struggling to teach myself Haitian and German by systematically read-ing a little New Testament most days.

One result of this was that I shifted my present real-ity to include the reality of the scripture. It was so immedi-ate to me, and much more present than the world outside my home.

If you were to ask me how things were, I may just as easily have told you Rebecca and Isaac just died, or the women were at the tomb, or David let Saul go once again. I thought about it during my day, much the same as I think about the activities of my family.

When Herod had the babies killed I cry like I had lost one of my own.

When Jesus asks a question: "Which is easier to say - 'Your sins are forgiven, or to say 'Get up and walk?'" I think on the answer back and forth, and draw conclusions as if he had singled me out for a response. I laugh every time Rhoda leaves Peter standing outside the door.

I read aloud every difficult name in Chronicles, rolling the sounds around in my mouth, finding it easier every time.

I blush for Peter when he hears the cock crow and realizes what he's done.

I compare my Tom to Boaz, and conclude that Ruth and I are fortunate women indeed-

## ~ *Forty* ~

Shell...
She has never had a shy moment.
She has never bragged.
She has never wished ill upon another.

She sees nothing to be afraid of—
Spiders, snakes, mice.
She hears nothing to be afraid of—
Thunder, growling, crashes.
She learns nothing to be afraid of—
Bankruptcies, wars, crime.

A disaster of complications and conditions
With a pure and simple heart.
She arouses others to greater lives
Without a word.
She makes her way in this world
With no example or chart to follow.

She is what I want to be when I grow up.

By early December 2003, Shelly seems to be finding new ways to frighten me with her stomach bloating, foul diarrhea and occasional fevers. Things are manageable during the day but night brings on fears and I worry about every move she makes.

Her face seems puffy, but it may just be the light, I tell myself. Her stomach fluid is black, but that's come and gone before.

Instead of seeming to be in pain, her mood is sweet and loving, and makes me watch her all the more closely, knowing how much I'd miss her if she died. I listen to her breathing as she sleeps. I take her temperature more often than is sensible and then take it again in case the thermometer was inaccurate. She wants to be left alone a lot, cuddled under her blanket. I let her, but want to pick her up and hold her. I am afraid she will die and I won't be holding her. Beyond imagining.

About the middle of the month, I realize Shell's neck seems swollen, especially on her right side. I take her to see Doctor Fulkerson, our pediatrician, and he's not sure what is going on either. Perhaps scar tissue has blocked up the passage of fluid that should be draining and he worries about her airway being blocked off. We confer with Columbus Children's and they say words like "stroke". I get blood labs drawn at our local hospital and go home. All discussions of what can be done in the hospital come to the same conclusion- nothing can be done for this child without veins.

Christmas is approaching, and I keep watch on Shell's racing pulse, as if knowing the rate, I can somehow will it to keep beating.

I call Carolyn Doran, a friend of Columbus Don's. I want to prepare her in case Shell dies, so she will go in person to tell Don. I don't think I could tell him bad news over the phone.

Shell's breathing is loud, wheezing past the swollen neck and bluish lips. Her face is puffy and she sleeps a lot. When she is awake her breathing is rapid and I find it hard to even give her up to Tom for short breaks, my mind and heart staying wrapped around her. I pray for her breathing to ease, for her not to suffocate, for her to have peace if she is to die. Her breathing eases- Thank you, Lord.

We prepare for the holiday, even as life revolves around the Redhead; still the calls from my far-off family in turmoil, still life going on here, wrapping gifts and baking cookies. As is my custom, I take Dr. Fulkerson, who is also a neighbor, some cookies for the holidays and he asks about Shell, worried she's getting so bad. He calls in Hospice and they arrive at our messy house the next morning, Christmas Eve.

Meeting Shelly, the hospice worker expresses certainty that she is arriving for the end stage. Shell's breathing is loud, even in the next room. Her blood pressure is a whopping 40/10. She is as weak as a kitten and looking like death warmed over.

Congestive heart failure seems to be what is going to take her, after all. I sign the necessary papers, listen to the reassuring discussions of comfort drugs and I'm grateful for the kind of support hospice brings.

We still have family over for our usual Christmas Eve traditions. The birth story from Luke, read by Tom, reduces me to tears. Everything reduces me to tears, it seems. But we also find joy, and I am glad for the family's chance to spend a last time with the Bean.

We wake on Christmas morning to the quiet miracle of easier breathing and less swelling. Shell's color seems better and I'm not as fearful for her life. Shell always lives—she just does. She doesn't know how to die. And slowly, with many frightful setbacks, her stubborn spirit fights its way back.

She retains a weakness after this that we'd not seen before, but she goes about her quiet life much as before. Finally, after many weeks, she earns the "I survived Hospice" tee shirt; once again sweetly failing to do what is expected of her.

I measure stomach fluids. I measure and measure and measure, all through the day. I'm not sure exactly why; and I keep a scrupulously messy record of every drop in old notebook, page after page.

I detach the bag from her stomach tube and replace it with an empty one... The fluid ranges from every shade of blue and green and yellow, to a dark-almost-black, that

165

signals blood in the gut.

I draw it out of the bag with a 60cc syringe and before long I possess a strange expertise in counting by 60's... 60-120-180-240-300-360-420-480-540-600. Numbers and I don't normally mix, but I practice simple addition by tallying up her amounts every night.

Sometimes her output is low... 200 - 300 range, and sometimes it gets up around 1000 - 1400 for no good reason at all. It's not as if I've changed how much I feed her. The input stays the same unless there's a very good reason. And it's not like the exercise she gets alters from day to day.

Nevertheless, the quantity varies so much I can never be sure, and I keep a close eye on her bag, bulging from excess, or lying flat for hours... and measure.

## ~ *Forty One* ~

*"Greater love has no one than this...that he lay
down his life for his friends." John 15:13*

~ * ~

We think it means dying, but it may not always mean
dying.
To lay down one's life for a friend—may just mean
living.

Ask a caregiver...

Wistfully missing out on travel,
Dinner dates, plans for tomorrow and forever-
Sending regrets for showers and weddings and
family reunions and parties
Losing friends piece by piece-even strong ties slip-
ping from neglect...

Float away, normal world.
Love also makes this an easy choice.

Even from the first, while Shell was on the IV, we
couldn't leave her unattended. Her sleeping patterns were
always off, days and nights mixed up.

We gave up on a bedroom and haven't had one
since. Instead, we pulled out a single mattress every night
next to her bed and I got up and down to see to her needs
or get her a toy.

No Bedroom
The advantages:

Never, ever have a cluttered, messy bedroom.

Using rooms for other things, a music room,
A library-

Closer cuddling on a single mattress.
Feeling the joys of hippy-like freedom.
Dog alarm clocks, drool style.

The disadvantages:

No bedroom to hide our messiness-
Sneaking around like teenagers for
private time.
Really, really small bed.
Feeling like a vagabond hippy.
Dog alarm clocks, drool style.

## ~ Forty-Two ~

Imagine being twenty years old and never having taken a bite of food.

Sometimes, I thought I could entice Shell to just try something, maybe something sweet. I'd take a candy cane, at Christmas time, and rub it along her teeth when she would let me get near her mouth. She showed no surprised pleasure at the sweet taste, and maybe that's a good thing, considering how impossible it was to brush her teeth.

When Shelly was born, and first put on an IV for nutrition, the nurses would try to keep up bottle feeding her, but she was so sick so often she either never developed a desire for it, or just lost the desire along the way.

I always thought the smell of pizza or chocolate would make her curious to try some. I spent a lot of time demonstrating how all the rest of us ate, having her feel the process - reminiscent of scenes from the Helen Keller story, but Shelly remained uninterested.

Even now, I 'let' her feed me small things I'm eating while holding her, like M&M's or potato chips, or berries. She must think I'm some sort of freak to do such a thing, and she giggles as she shoves the piece into my mouth, feels my cheeks for the chewing, and my throat for the swallowing. Swallowing anything solid is so alien to Shelly, I'm afraid she could aspirate into her lungs if she tried.

Though, once upon a time, when she was about ten or eleven years old, I sat with her, drinking some ginger ale, and she felt it go up to my lips, so I put it up to her lips too.

For whatever reason at the moment, she didn't fight it, but let a few drops in. Very excited, I tried all sorts of liquids and she would even hold the cup herself for a few seconds while taking a tiny sip. I don't know where things would have gone from there if she'd not gotten a septic line a couple of months later, and spent a full week in the hospital. On returning home, she refused to try another drink and never allowed one near her lips again.

Eating no food, on the other hand, meant there were no cavities. The question came up from time to time of how I managed to brush her teeth. It mortified me to say we didn't. We didn't because she wouldn't let us.

Shelly would clamp her teeth together firmly and even the dentist would have to make wedges with tongue depressors to pry open her mouth, several people assisting to holding her fighting, squirming, strong body. Eventually the only way any dental work could be done at all was to put her to sleep for the procedure.

Still - no cavities, Mama!

Today, Shelly turns twenty-one—legal age for you and me. For Shell it's just another day.

She gets a present. It's a video seat, a soft cush-ioned flat thing. It folds up, and you would normally sit on the floor and let it support your back. She loves it. To her it's an interesting thing to bend over her knees while lying on the bed and it is a pleasure to watch how it makes her smile all day. She likes it well enough to allow it bed-space, instead of sending it to the floor with the more tem-porary toys.

But today she turns twenty-one—the day known in America as a turning point to adulthood. Usually making these 'new-adults' act less responsibly, rather than more so, it is often celebrated with binge drinking or smoking in front of a parent, or clubbing till one is clobbered.

Of course before this, there is the magic of turning 18, old enough to die as a soldier, old enough to vote, old enough to be in trouble with a "minor" even if you are barely older than the minor.

But there are still cross-over points when you turn

twenty-one, and for my son, who is still three days away from that goal, it will seem like the word "adult" finally applies without question.

What was I doing at twenty-one? I think about this on and off during the day, as I buy shiny silver balloons for my little girl who is hardly bigger than an eight-year-old, as I hang them on her bed she's consigned to for life, as I fill her feeding machine, knowing she'll never taste birthday cake.

I was planning my wedding at her age - the wedding to take place only a month away. I was in love with my Tom. I was working for a landscaper, having melted out of Art College in the ever-so-foreign city of Boston.

I had a horse. I drove a car. I took long walks in the woods. I was unsure of many things, like how to find God, or if I would have a career or only a job, or if I could keep some of my parents' values and still find my own.

Shelly is doing none of that. She's aware of none of those options I'd taken for granted. She's living like no one I've ever known. She will never have a boyfriend or get married. She will never have children or drive a car, or make life-decisions. She will never hear of binge drinking, or condoms, or checking accounts. She will never have a roommate from college, a pen-pal, a cheerleading squad or a favorite TV show. She will never text a friend, have a special ring-tone, or talk on the phone for hours. She will never have a favorite pizza topping, or try on high heels or get a speeding ticket.

*How do you make your way in the world when your way is not like the rest of the world?*
*You just do.*
*Happy Birthday, Dearest Shelly Bean.*

People have asked me if I ever wondered how God could have let this happen to an innocent child—bad gut, blindness, deafness.

This is the child I know. If she was sighted and hear-Ing, and had no physical ailments, I would never have met her.

I have her because of these issues, and Shelly is the child she is.


Not a sighted child.
Not a hearing child.
Not a child who can eat normally.
I would never wish difficulties on a child,
But I don't ever wish Shelly was not Shelly.
Perfectly Shelly.


"Tom... I love this child."
"I know you do."
"Tom, she's so beautiful! Don't you think so?"
"Yes. She's beautiful."
"She loves her Mama."
"Yes, she does."

## ~ Forty-Three ~

*G*uardianship Day.

The *day* finally came. It had been put off twice since her birthday in November, but the date held up for January 26th, and I was more excited to see this day than reality warranted.

In reality, it made little difference in Shelly's life, or mine. When she needed surgeries in the past, the doctors and I made the decision, and told the social services, and they signed for it. They weren't about to argue against her needs, of course.

And knowing I now had the ability to make her financial decisions was a moot point. I'd been doing so with temporary guardianship since she turned twenty-one.

It was just the finality of it. Not quite an adoption, but sort of the same feeling. It gave a more permanent feeling to our lives together.

"I am the boss of you! I am the boss of you!" I chanted to her unhearing ears after returning from court - knowing full well nobody bosses this redhead around.

With the change of dates, I had been thinking the time may have changed also, but with my usual laid-back attitude, didn't look into it until eight o'clock on the morning of the trial. The paper with a time for the court got lost, (again because of my laid-back attitude), so I had to call the courthouse for the information.

As it turns out, they can't give you that kind of information. All the clerk could legally tell me was that most activity started at nine o'clock a.m. Mind you, I'd started my day pretty late already, looking for the lost papers, and still had a shower to take, so I arrived at the courthouse two minutes late.

Upstairs, I found two other women waiting outside

the courtroom, who told me it was standing-room only in there. I checked inside, hoping to see our social worker, but they were doing roll call. It took a few minutes of listening to realize they were gathering their juries for the day, and I could go out and wait with the two women. Mornings are not my best think-tank times, believe me.

So began my lovely day of waiting. I'm not being facetious here, I really had one of the most enjoyable days I've had in a long, long time.

Right away we three women hit it off, and talked for the next two hours or more, involving different people who came in and sat, or people passing by to the courtroom knowing one or the other of us.

One of the women was there to get guardianship of her husband, who had suffered from a brain hemorrhage in December, and was now in rehab at the VA hospital. He is only in his mid-50's and I know they must have been making all the normal plans couples make about retirement and their future on the other side of child raising. Then in such a sudden moment, life is changed and changed forever, and the foggy path to coping is not yet revealed, being slowly and reluctantly stepped on in strange places like a courtroom.

The other woman was also there for guardianship, but of her sister who was in a care facility and unable to manage her own affairs.

We talked about everything under the sun. The birth of our babies, doctors we knew and admired, fears and sorrows, the love of Kentucky, poetry and poets, possibilities and hopes, our grown children, the way things were, the way things are and the way things will someday be.

I guess it's all the things women talk about when they begin and things flow. At another time, on another day, perhaps we would have been wrapped up in ourselves and never have gone past a nod of our heads. I wonder why it's so - sometimes a crowed elevator gets to the bottom with everyone smiling and chatting, and other times with everyone just enduring the ride.

The social worker for Shelly was also the worker for the woman needing spousal guardianship, and we'd seen her flying in and out of the courtroom in her familiar distracted way. Occasionally she would stop to get us updated with what she knew, apologizing for our wait. I told her to not worry about Shelly's case being heard first, because I was enjoying the company I found myself in.

At any rate, I was called in first. Shelly's lawyer, Mr. D., our former mayor, was there, as was the lawyer for me, who I didn't remember meeting beforehand. Everyone was relaxed and pleasant as the jury got seated, and both lawyers spoke instructions to them, saying similar things.

Mr. D. spoke of why they have a jury decide this sort of thing - they don't want a system where groups of lawyers sit around and make decisions about people's lives. They both said that even though there are many days, as apposing council, they disagree on the desired outcome, this was one of those times they were in complete agreement about what should happen concerning Shelly.

Both had kind words and made the jury feel that even though they wouldn't be doing something dramatic like locking up a bad guy, what they would be doing by giving us guardianship was more important and the right thing to do and they would go home feeling good about what had resulted from their day on the jury.

I was called as the first "witness." I'd only done this once before, for a child custody case involving a friend, and I've not been speaking much for the past five years. Literally, I've not been speaking much, in my small world here with Shelly, and most of the time, that was to the same people who know me well.

At least I didn't feel nervous. I was enjoying it like an adventure, and any chance to tell someone about my girl, is joy to me. I had brought pictures, and they went around to the jury, and later to the rest of the courtroom. It showed Shelly as a beautiful happy girl, and I'm sure everyone there felt it must be a treasure to know this child.

Every face on the jury looked kind, and every question from the lawyers was encouraging, asked with a smile. It's hard to know how much to say, how much is needed and I tried to not detail too much.

The social worker spoke next, verifying she and Shelly's doctor, and an independent representative from Comprehensive Care, agreed concerning Shelly's need for full guardianship. There was the closing from the lawyers and the jury retired to a back room. My normal life experiences did not include thinking, *the jury retired to the back room.* What a day!

I needed to leave the courtroom for a few minutes as the previous jury gave their verdict, and so had a chance to speak again with the women in the hall. The one caring for a sister had said she wished to be a lawyer in another life, so she was paying close attention to the proceedings.

When I went back in, it was only after the shortest of deliberations, and we had been awarded full guardianship. I hadn't doubted we would get her, as I could see no one in the wings waiting for their chance to snatch her from us, but it was still a sweet moment.

Several jury members hugged me on the way out. Others shook my hand, each saying kindnesses, and wishing us the best. I went up to the judge to sign papers, and she said, "God bless you all," which sentiment taped itself to my heart for the good of my soul.

The lawyers mentioned coming to visit sometime, the pictures made the rounds again, and the guard spoke gently, saying I'd made an impression. But it's not me who made the impression at all, I know.

It was the little redhead girl who couldn't even show

up for her big day - who changes lives and makes forever impressions on people's hearts.

And - I am the boss of her! I am the boss of her!

## ~ Forty-Four ~

My legs hurt from all the holding. I see thrombosis in my future, which is no future at all. I am so awkward in public that I blush during stuttered conversations. I return home in tears from the humiliation of being so stupid out there in the world. I withdraw more and more.

But my joy is right there at home - my joy is in the small hands holding mine as I sign - my joy is in the laugh delighting my wakeful nights - my joy is in the toss of red hair before a hug around my neck - my joy is in her warm comfort, and in knowing someone so unique and incredible as my Shell.

Shell—who knows nothing of outside storms and
stresses.
Shell—who lives perfectly in the moment
The very moment most of us miss every time.
Shell—whose emotions are unfeigned.
Shell—who never got the memo on holding grudges,
or faking friendship.
Shell—to whom greed is unheard of,
Whining is unthought of,
And lying is impossible-
Shell.

*"But the eyes are blind. One must look with the heart."*
*(Le Petit Prince)*

How ironic is it that one of the few people to really see me is a blind kid? I am invisible to the world and most hours of the day, even to my family who are out doing things in real-time.

I rarely go out. Once when I ventured into a bank, I

waited - the first one in line as the woman behind the counter kept busy, her head down. When she looked up, she saw only the man behind me, and waited on him. I stayed as she looked past to the next person, then I slipped out, abashed, almost driving home, errand unfinished.

On impulse, I took my car to the window and the same woman waited on me because she could see my car.

But The Bean *sees* me. She knows the tread of my feet across her room. She feels my throat when I laugh and laughs with me. She reaches a small hand up to my ear, though we both know she knows who I am.

She waits for me, and if someone else approaches, she feels them and then searches me out. She knows when I'm impatient and she becomes needier. She knows when I'm crying and feels for my tears. She gets jokes she never hears and chuckles.

She never sees what I see of me: homely, useless, and unkempt.

She doesn't eye my clothes from the day before and wonder how it's possible I'm wearing them again.

She never chides me to cut my hair fashionably...or holds my outdated glasses up for inspection.

She's not impressed when I put on make-up, or color my nails.

If I speak or am silent, if I sing on-key or off, if I struggle aloud with the same poem for days- she has no retort.

As long as I cut the tags from my shirts, I am safe from her inspection.

Shell has the eyes of the heart.

I am an often depressed optimist and Tom is a rarely depressed pessimist. It makes for an interesting viewpoint in our household.

My depressions can be hard and frightfully deep, but I have a vast and total confidenc in myself and others. I see huge visions of possibilities and don't see obstacles except as feathers to be blown away with a breath of chance and hope.

Tom is steady and keeps his mind clear, being sure of himself to do the right thing, and then doing it. His low moods soon clear as he lives more in the reality of the moment and sets his sights on things credibly attainable. At times he visits the wasteland of what can go wrong, delving into the 'what-if's' and 'buts' too much.

But he lets my mind soar, as long as he can. He lets me think I can visit France, or be in the Amazing Race, or rescue the world. When the time comes to break it to me that I'm a dreamer, he does it as gently as he can. I love him for that.

Tom was eighteen years old.
I was seventeen.
He came to my house and out of the blue, told me that he loved me.
Since then, every day
He has proven how much.

## ~ Forty-Five ~

Diarrhea smells -
Sending Tom to early coffee outside on the swing
Sending Isaiah to piano practice in the music room
Burying Laura's nose in a book
Burying dogs' noses into their beds
Leaving unanswered questions on students' frowns
Leaving its memory in sheets and blankets
Letting incense from India glow
Letting Shell delight in soap and bubbles.

Slowly, I began to change some things in my life. For one thing, I knew if I was going to continue being there for Shell, I couldn't keep holding her for so many hours a day. I gradually worked it down to three or four hours at a time, every evening.

Shell's world changed too, and as the meds took care of her anger, I had my sweet, happy, silly, funny red-head back once again. She played with the toys we'd give her, or make her way around the house searching out new playthings. We spent time out on the swing, even though it meant she was off the feeding machine, and she loved her bath times.

Who knows what she must have thought as she adjusted to our new life. Where were her teachers? Where were the rides to school? There were no ways to explain things to her, and I could only keep her entertained as much as possible there in her small universe.

We danced, we played, we tried to keep up on her words, but I found that the more she was stimulated when there was no end result for it, the more frustrating it was for her. Why learn to tie shoes when you're not going anywhere in them? Why learn new words for things you'll nev-

181

er be in contact with?

As Shell's world contracted, she became more satisfied with it. I realized the same thing was happening to me, too. I would wake up quietly content in the morning. I taught myself how to play the violin better, and practiced daily, taking on students which led to more students, which took me out of my isolation for small stretches of time.

I started reading classics in French, and began to write a novel. One day I had a sudden urge to try paper mache, and for about a year I created all sorts of fun and useless items. One day, just as suddenly as I began, I put the paper mache down, (right in the middle of a baby-sized cherub) and went off to search out my old set of pastels.

When my first results were satisfactory, I began to do pastels of people's pets for some additional money. The things I now had the time to do, I never would have been able to find the time for, if it was not for God and Shelly.

*And The Survey Says.*

The phone rang and my first impression was some 'cause' wanted money. As usual the voice rattled on too quickly to break in without being rude, and I wasn't in a rude mood.

The accent was strong, but the English easily understandable, and the woman sounded young. I soon heard enough to realize this was a survey I'd apparently answered questions to about six years ago, and they were doing a follow-up on our 'member of the household with special needs' who would now be twenty-one years of age.

So I stayed on the line. It was some official center of disease control or similar place taking the poll, and I happened to have the time right then.

**Woman:** As the person in question is now twenty-one years old, we would like to interview her about her home and life situation.

**Me**: Well, actually she is deaf and blind and doesn't speak, so that won't work out.

**Woman**: Okay- Let me check to see what to do now. Okay, I'd like to ask if there is any problem with my speaking with her directly.

**Me**: Yes, she's deaf and can't understand you.

**Woman**: So, are you saying she's hearing impaired?

**Me**: Yes, she's deaf. She can't hear.

**Woman**: Okay, let me check my notes on what to do. Sorry I was gone so long. I have it now. Will she like to speak to me now, or should I set up an appointment to relay the call?

**Me**: We can't relay the call, she won't understand you and she won't understand any of this. She just signs into my hands a limited world of signs.

**Woman**: Okay. Let me see what my notes say to do. I'm sorry I was gone so long. I have it now. You can answer for her and I will ask the questions as if I am talking to her.

**Me**: I guess we could do that.

At this point, the conversation was fairly ridiculous.

**Woman**: Are you receiving the care for your special needs you are entitled to?

**Me**: (the psychic for my daughter): Yes, I am.

**Woman**: Are you attending school or going to job training?

**Me**: No.

**Woman**: Would you like to be in school at this time?

**Me**: (pausing... Because really, I think Shell would like that). So I say yes.

**Woman**: Is anyone assisting you to be able to go to school at this time.

**Me**: No.

**Woman**: What was the last grade you completed?

**Me**: (After some calculating): The 6th grade, I guess.

**Woman**: (With a disapproving pause): Okay. On to another line of questions. Do you have a doctor you see for your special needs?

**Me:** Yes.

**Woman:** And have you gone to see this doctor in the past five months?

**Me:** No.

**Woman:** (With another disapproving pause) When was the last time you went to see your doctor?

**Me:** (forgetting I'm answering for Shelly) Actually, I only speak with the doctor on the phone.

**Woman:** But you said you have a doctor to see you.

**Me:** (Not wanting to explain the doctor can't do much for Shell in person) Well, yes, but not in person.

**Woman:** Let me check my notes and change all that. Okay, sorry I was gone so long. And do you go to the dentist on a regular basis?

**Me:** No.

**Woman:** (Yet another, even more obvious, disapproving pause). You don't go to the dentist?

**Me:** Well, actually she used to go, but she never eats and so, doesn't get cavities, and they can't get into her mouth without knocking her out and she has no lines for an IV.

**Woman:** (Not listening to my explanation as it wasn't on her list) And do you have insurance?

At this point I was starting to feel like a very uncaring, neglectful proxie voice for my child.

**Woman:** So would you say you are: Very satisfied, satisfied, not very satisfied, or not at all satisfied with the following:

The level of care you are receiving?

**Me:** Satisfied. (Shelly would let me know if she wasn't very satisfied or was not at all satisfied, for sure)

**Woman:** With the situation in your homelife?

**Me:** Satisfied.

**Woman:** With your job? Oh no. You don't have a job. With your level of medical care?

**Me:** Very satisfied.

At this point we're both just sounding pathetic.

Then came the clincher:

**Woman:** For my final question, would you say you were: Very happy, happy, not very happy, or very unhappy with your life?

(At this point I burst into tears).

**Me:** (when I could speak again) I ask you, what would you say? How can I say if she is happy? She is content.

She would be happy if she could go swimming this summer in the ocean, if she could ride a bike around town, if she could have friends over for a movie night, if she could drive to a store and go shopping, if she could text-message her boyfriend and stay out late nights. If she even knew these things existed, maybe she'd be happy doing them if she could. But she can't, and is so unaware of them that she is content.

**Woman:** (Unable to color outside of the lines of her survey): So would you say she is very happy, happy or un-happy?

**Me:** Yes.

~ * ~

So, I took a chance and got a dream dog. A Rott-weiller puppy. I was afraid to get just any Rottie. It would have to be well-bred and from great parents, and raised from birth around people. Just because I've always adored the breed, didn't mean I'd know how to deal with one having a bad temperament. But a well-bred dog would mean an expensive dog, which was out of the question. I firmly believe in rescuing dogs from pounds.

So, this became the irony. I got a perfect, wonder-ful, sweet, smart, dear, loving, assertive Rottie because of Shelly. And because of this Rottie, Shelly had to move from the house she knew so well.

185

Life is like that sometimes. God is like that sometimes.

~ * ~

Eleanor is the woman we got our pup from and she has a special child. When she heard from my dear friend Rhea how nuts I've always been for Rotties, she took everything into consideration.

In the first place, we didn't have, and likely never would have, the purchase price for this amazing dog, coming from a long line of show champions. And we also had a special child. Special children draw us closer to others, and Carl entered our lives for only what was already put into vet bills.

Eleanor may never know how much she blessed us, and changed our lives.

I named him Carl even before Tom and Nathaniel went to South Carolina to pick him up. I always loved the Carl Book for children, and his first 'mom,' Eleanor, said he sure had a "Carl" personality.

Then the land sold. The eighty acres and home we'd been renting for over eighteen years managed to sell to a man who was afraid of big dogs.

He said he'd fix up the old house, raise the rent, start building nearby developments, and we could stay there after getting rid of our Rottie.

Hum-m-m... What a bargain. We started house hunting.

Tom and I are in our early fifties and have never bought a house. I'm hoping we never buy another.

I cried all the time about having to move. So there was all that to deal with—the tissues, the heaving sighs, the pretending to be *okay* with it all, the tissues again. I had raised my kids in that house and buried dear animals, planted my rose garden and many, many trees now towering overhead. There were tears and tissues for everything and every memory—the little guys taking baths, climbing into the tree fort, having school in the classroom, falling asleep while reading in bed, putting in the goat, feeding the rabbits and horses.

I tried and failed to bring up memories of the kids making their beds, or taking out trash—but still, many sweet memories.

Tom has always wanted to buy a house. He's wanted to make the kind of decisions only homeowners could make—like whether to pay the mortgage at the beginning of the month or at the end, and whether he wanted to go into debt over new windows or new gutters, and whether he wanted to spend years perfecting the place and getting it just the way he wanted it and then selling it to someone else.

To me, renting was just fine. Owning a place didn't have the same lure to my army brat soul as it did to Tom, but it sure seemed like the time had come to buy.

And buy we did.

Just for the heck of it:

Thoughts on Buying a House.

#1. Don't.

If you disregard #1, then what can I tell you? You're not going to listen to me anyway. Go ahead- Buy your house. Create havoc. Buy into the concept of ownership besting renter-ship. Take the tiny teeny pictures of a dream home from the back pages of your newspaper and picture your tiny teeny self - walking around the tiny teeny rooms inside.

But when a pipe leaks, it's "yours" and when the basement floods from said pipe, it's also "yours," and when you find a solid gold watch the last owners left behind, well, that's "yours" too.

Our vocabulary expanded, though I'm not sure I learned every new word exactly the way Tom did, what with all the crying and the tissues. What I did glean from it all was this:

**Realtor:** This could possibly be a friend—apparently everyone you know either is a realtor (for real), or does it on the side, or has a relative who "does real estate", or at least "hopes to get into real estate someday".

But I can't get past the concern I'm saying the word wrong. Some days I put three syllables in, such as 'Reel-a-tor'. Some days I'm sophisticated and go with the two syllables 'Reel-tor'. Whichever I use I'm sure it's wrong, and think about it while my realtor is actually talking about "important" things, so I miss out on many explanations, and she has to repeat herself endlessly.

**Bank:** I thought I knew the basics of a bank, but when you buy a house what you 'know' all goes out the window. There is much about your bank you don't know.

For instance, they may not be the ones you want or need to handle your house buying. You may have been with them for the past 30 years, but when you go to buy a house it's as if they never met you. They pretend you just got here from Mars and may hop a spaceship as soon as you get your loan.

So, they do a background check, and then another and another. I believe it's based on every third phone call you make to ask if the bank is still in business, it's been so long since they've gotten back with you.

At some point you find that your perfect credit rating isn't so perfect anymore, although you've now put off any major purchases, including replacing the refrigerator that picked this very time to die. You've started using an old camping cooler, stuffed with ice, milk and questionable bologna to avoid messing up your credit rating, but still somehow it took a nosedive.

Come to find out, every time anyone even peeks into your secret credit rating score, you get punished by default. It seems in the midst of a high storm at sea, every rocking move of your little rowboat gets noticed by the powers that be. Forget bailing, it's too late by the time you even know it's happened.

**Assessors:** Not to be confused with Appraisers. At least not to be confused with them several times a day like I was. Okay... Now that I look at them again, I don't know the difference, and apparently there's a *big* difference- a big enough difference to cause a frustrated look to come over the realtor's face every time you confuse them and she has to explain their jobs all over again. Now is it Real-a-tor, or Real-tor?

So, let's say it's 'Assessors' I'm thinking about. From what I've gathered, after you've done all the searching of tiny teeny houses pictured in your newspaper, or real estate fliers (which suddenly multiply by the hundreds in your mailbox right at this opportune time) or scan the internet way into the night, the bank sends out to the desired house a person you've never met and aren't likely to meet, to give an opinion of the "real" cost of your dream home.

He has a set of rules to go by. For instance, if your house is as old as you are, its crap. So it won't appraise for as much as a cardboard cutout of a house that is 15 minutes old. Neither will you, if you want to know the truth. Age is a minus.

If your house has, say, indoor plumbing-well, that's a plus. And it nitpicks from there. If it has unbroken windows, or floor joists, or right-of-way access to the nearest road, well more plus, plus, plus!

Mold is never a plus. Mold is a minus, as is a strong odor of cat urine. These assessors/appraisers are very strict.

Then it's location, location... Well, you know the rest. Here in Kentucky we're measured by how close we are to Lexington, the largest city. Although when you get right down to it, everything actually rests on how close you are to the nearest Walmart. If you build in the Walmart parking lot, forget about it. You can't afford the mortgage.

Then the final test.Does your dream house cost about as much as the house down the road which sold last week? And by "about" I mean to the last penny, not higher, not lower.

The "comparable" house must have the same amount of space, just as many floors, X amount of same windows, be the same age and personality of the one you're buying, and must have sold within a half hour of yours. Sounds impossible, right?
I already told you not to buy a house, so don't complain to me about impossible.

By now, you are coveting the "comparable" house, and yours will never again look as good to you as that one, which is, alas, already sold.

So those are the guidelines, but from our extremely limited experience, I believe the assessor/appraiser actually goes by what he likes.

Thumbs down if he doesn't like log cabins, or thatched roofs, or underground windowless dwellings.

Thumbs up if it reminds him of his grandmother's house, or has a sweet puppy playing in the yard, or has electricity After all, appraiser/assessors are people too.

## ~ Forty-Six ~

*I* worried all along about what a move would do to Shelly. I had assumed I knew what God thought on the subject of Shelly, and had also assumed, wrongly again, how Shell would react to such a change.

I thought God would never ask it of Shell to move. Maybe I hoped He'd never ask it of me, and I saw Shell as the most obvious reason we'd stay put. I thought with all she'd been through since birth, being in a stable environment would be essential for her and the angels would plead her (my) case.

But as the move went forward in spite of my misgivings, I decided not to think of how it would affect her. I just put all the preparations into place to see she would have the least disruptive disruption I could give her.

That meant her schedule went on schedule, no exceptions. She was unaware of my packing, and I never moved anything she was accustomed to finding, or packed when I should have been holding or taking care of her. Packing took a lot longer, but it was worth it.

The packing process, after living in the same house for almost twenty years, is one I'd not care to repeat twenty years from now, though this would likely be the worst move, after raising so many kids and still having all their lives to sort out.

I guess I was thinking I'd never have to do it - that the leggos would somehow disappear over time through the missing floorboards in the attic room, the huge bunk beds Tom had made would just gradually become used by grandchildren, the packages of shrimp I'd impulsively bought from a traveling refrigerated truck 18 years ago would be served up for a festive occasion one of these days. Dealing proactively with the 'stuff' was something I had the luxury

191

of avoiding up till now.

On the bright side, I found a box of old photos I had even forgotten I was missing, and mementos from when Tom and I were dating, and more nail clippers than I ever thought possible.

I started with the books, filling box after box to the point of straining hernias. Then to the upstairs rooms, sorting, filing, tossing, sorting, filing, tossing... reminiscing, crying and more sorting.

By some standards, Tom and I are packrats. Not the kind you see on TV, who save everything they come in contact with and eventually have to live in the tree house because it's roomier than home. No, we're just the average kind of pack rats. We save stuff for sentimental reasons, like 3 cans of really good black beer from the early 70's, back when we drank beer. One can was mysteriously empty though unopened, and the other two were surprisingly full, though kind of nasty from years in the attic.

Crumbled flower petals, stones with long lost meanings, old rosary beads from a catholic childhood, most of which got saved again and moved. I told Tom our kids would just have to throw it out when we're gone.

We also save stuff we might use again. Old light fixtures we may someday scrape the paint off and find a place for, yarn that sure looked good in the 80's and may end up in another unnecessary afghan, way too many electronic gizmos we're not sure about enough to just toss out. It could be we'd need one to charge a VCR re-winder, if VCR's ever come back en vogue, or power a kid's remote control car, broken in so many pieces we need a separate box for it, in case we find the time to repair it. I debated so long with myself whether to risk Tom's dismay and toss out his 8-track tapes, a thing I'd threatened to do for years. I was so happy to find them moldy beyond salvaging, getting me off the hook for deep-sixing them.

I found the early part of packing was the easy part.

Not a big deal to paper up the dishes, load up the pots and pans, find boxes for clothes. The hard part comes at the end, when all the sensible stuff is taken care of, and what's left is a bunch of stupid, stupid stuff.

What to do with the bit of a once tall candle, the post-it notes you may wish you had someday, the stray magnet with a seashell attached, the pot-less pot-lid that possibly fits something else, the box of aquarium charcoal for fish we'll never have, the too small dog harness - too chewed up to return, and not chewed up enough to toss out. In the end, a lot of stuff just got put in a box marked *Crap*.

The fatigue creeps in after days and weeks of packing, and then waiting for the bank to determine our fate while we live out of boxes, not remembering which one now contains the wrapping paper, and which one has the dogs' brushes.

There finally comes a day when it's late at night, and you're standing in the middle of an echoing room, staring stupidly at the latest two things in your hands. Your mind is so tired it is registering in slow motion the objects in need of a decision. In the one hand is a quarter, and you can't think of where the change jar is, so you let it fall through your fingers into the black plastic trash bag you're hauling from room to room. It hits the bag but rolls out and across the floor, and you don't care. You're too tired to care. Let the new owner get rich...

In the other hand is something else you slowly identify, and it sets up a conflict in your mind—to save, to toss—to save, to toss? It's a band-aid with only one little spot of blood. Too tired to decide, you shove it into a pocket.

All the worrying about 'the Move' and how Shelly might react to it intensified as the time approached. I wanted to make it happen with as little confusion and disruption of her life as possible, but my expectation was that it was going to be just horrible.

I would lie awake at night picturing her being angry and wanting answers I couldn't give her. I imagined her getting there and never settling down - instead roaming around the house trying to figure out where she was for weeks on end. I pictured her being exposed to new germs and added stress, sickening her quickly, and I would live with endless guilt for somehow letting this happen to her. I felt I let her down - somehow I should have made it possible for her to live peacefully and instead I allowed all this chaos into her world.

Added to the Shelly-factor was my sorrow at leaving our home, so I made the decision Shell and I would be the last ones to leave. I wanted to know the house was empty and clean, and I needed the chance to say 'goodbye'. Goodbye to the house, the trees, the land, the pets' graves, the stream, the sky viewed from the backyard, the places I knew so well.

When you've been someplace for so long, you know just where the moon travels, just which way the wind blows, just how long the day should feel, just when to expect the seasons. It's all jumbled around when you move to somewhere new, and even though it's still all the natural things of the world, you have to re-learn the distance to the stars, and what constitutes a big storm and which birds migrate past. 'Goodbye' was very hard for me.

Of major difficulty was moving Shelly's water bed. We planned and re-planned how we could get her up on the morning of the last day, and find helpers to somehow drain and dismantle the bed, load it on the truck, drive the hour to our new home, set it back up, and fill it.

This would ideally take place while I somehow entertained Shelly all day which would mean she was already off schedule. It also meant I could not get anything else done for the last moving day. Moving never goes smoothly, and the chaos theory always evokes privileges at the wrong moment.

In the first place, we weren't able to find the kind of helpers who could fit our schedule, so Tom planned to do it himself. Adding to extra labor time was the hour drive to the new house and two hour return trip to retrieve Shell and me, plus the recliner I would have been using to hold her. It would be late getting her settled and hooked up.

The biggest obstacle was getting the waterbed filled with warm water from the new house's smaller water heater. It would take a long time, and Tom kept coming up with possible solutions. They all seemed too extreme to me. He wanted to fill a barrel of water several days in advance so it would be at least room temperature, and somehow get it to the second story landing so the hose could run downstairs to Shell's room. Finding the right kind of barrel, getting the water upstairs, worrying about leaking and other details were driving us to interesting levels of stress.

After having an actual argument, something we don't ever do, especially over something as small as where the dog's fence would go, I decided we'd have to disrupt Shelly's life a bit more to make it all work. We ended up moving the water bed two days in advance, when Tom could have help, and it would have plenty of time to fill with warm water. For the two nights before the move, we set up the air mattress in the place of Shelly's bed and put her toys exactly as they were normally found, and just acted like it was as normal as anything we've ever done. Shelly was surprised, got in and out several times, tried to unplug the air, and eventually just settled in.

In truth, it was a rough two days for her. She had been doing a strange thing lately of running fevers at random times of the day and having a lot of diarrhea. The fevers were gone, and I continually had to keep bundling blankets around her to keep her temperature at the 'alive' mark. She was used to the warm water bed, and air mattresses can suck the life out of you if you get cold.

The diarrhea hadn't stopped, and I don't know if that air mattress will ever be usable again.

The day of the move was a Sunday, and Tom went to a nearby early church service. We were still trying to wrap up the last bits of our lives, going from a big house to one somewhat smaller. There were things we couldn't fit, and we were not sure what we would do without them. In order to get to the new house in daylight so the dogs could check out the surroundings, we left things undone for the time being and loaded up.

Tom drove the loaded truck, pulling a borrowed trailer. I followed in the jeep with Shelly, and the four nervous, excited dogs in the rear, each trying to out-drool the others all over the back of my head. I had insisted on them being with me for the ride, so they wouldn't spend it worrying about where I was. Tom had the two yowling cats that I had tricked into carriers, and two cages of birds. We were a traveling circus for sure - all we lacked were the elephants.

Though I didn't know it then, that ride would be Shelly's last time in a car. She perked up when I signed to her that she would be going for a ride, and she only gradually lost steam as we made the hour's drive to our new home. Getting out, I started to lead her by the hand to the door, but she faltered after a few steps and I carried her into the warmed water bed.

She was more than content to stay in her room, where we had placed everything as near as possible to her former situation. I would lead her into the bathroom or carry her out to the swing, but even though she knew it was a new place; she chose to ignore the change. She was too weak to really care.

## ~ Forty-Seven ~

*"What are you trying to say?"*

*"In one of the stars I shall be living. In one of them I shall be laughing. And so it will be as if all the stars were laughing, when you look at the sky at night. You - only you - will have stars that can laugh!"*

*"And he laughed again."*

*(Le Petit Prince)*

How I love this child! She draws us to her with her infectious giggling. She wakes us up in the night when she finds a toy that blares out a siren and a loud "Intruder! Intruder!" and we lie there laughing at her, happy to wake for such a pleasure.

She gets a sweet sweaty smell in her hair, like a small child, and I can't get enough of breathing her in...

She rebels against unexplained authority and I am so proud of her it brings me to tears...

She flips back her hair, unaware of how cute it is or that anyone is watching.

She makes decisions for her own reasons of just exactly where every single toy in her bed should be: which ones should be taken to the end of the bed and dropped to the floor through the wooden rails, and which should be dropped to the side of the bed.

She laughs every single time we pretend to crack an egg over her head or knee—(thank you, Julie)—even when she's weak and tired.

She is a wonder to me. She makes the whole world different from what it ever was or could have been before. How I love this child!

Some days are hard - some days are really hard.

~ * ~

Today, my son Isaiah is getting married in Minnesota and I don't get to be there for it. I don't get to leave Shell and go with Tom to celebrate this and as many chances as I've had in the past many years to get used to missing out on things, this one hurts the bitterly anyway.

I explained to Isaiah on the phone that I don't have anyone I could leave Shell with, and I don't know if he believes me. It is his wedding, after all. But this son I love with all my heart must know I'd never miss out unless I had to- he must know my heart was breaking.

Today I just want to be there. I don't want to be giving suppositories and cleaning up the results. I don't want to be checking supplies, and adding food, and crushing pills, and measuring stomach fluids.

I want to be putting on a dress I would have spent hours picking out just for this occasion. I want to find a few moments alone with him to talk and hug. I want to watch Stacia get ready in her lovely gown and tell her how I have been praying for her all her life. I want to dance a mother-son dance at his reception. I want to relax and spend time with her family.

Tom goes, and opens his cell phone so I can hear the ceremony it as it happens. He misses me, but doesn't make me feel awful about not going. Going was not an option. We'll have another party here in a month with the newly-weds, and all their friends from this area will be here, too. I cling to that thought.

Some days are just hard.

## ~ Forty Eight ~

As if to make up for all the damage it would cause in those few days of winter, the ice storm of late January 2009 was gorgeous beyond belief. Crystal jewels on every surface and diamonds studding every branch of every bending tree, lovely to the eyes.

Tom went to Lexington that snowy Tuesday afternoon to pick up a missionary from Tanzania who would be using one of the vehicles from our missionary-aid effort. In mid-town he hit a loose manhole cover and the jeep ended up in a nearby garage waiting for parts. Thus, Tom was stranded in Lexington at our son's house for the night. Not a bad deal, spending the sweet time with our little grandson.

Shelly and I had our normal night. She hadn't been feeling great but, of course, insisted on finishing our time together by clearing off the couch cushions and dropping the pens on the hutch counter from their delicately balanced positions to the floor. I hovered over her every move, supporting when needed.

We woke to find the electricity out and the trees heavy with ice, crashing branches in the yard making it a real hazard to just step out for wood. Shell's water bed was still holding warmth, but I knew it wouldn't last, so I hurried to get an alternate situation set up for her.

Our faithful woodstove in the main room would be our life-line, so I brought in and stacked up as much split wood as I could find room for. I also plugged in our landline phone, but all phone service was gone by night, and my cell phone was almost out of bars.

I dragged a single mattress, well covered in blankets and sheets, close enough to the woodstove to be warm, but far enough away to be safe. Then I brought Shell in and placed her on the bed, expecting a rebellion.

The beginning of an illness kept her quiet, and she played with her pile of purses and binders as I cleaned the house and pulled our mattress into the room too. Everything still seemed possible, but it was a struggle to remember that light switches don't work at the flick of a hand. I began a puzzle on the table so I could watch Shelly, whose pump had been running on battery all this time.

Tom managed to get home by 6pm, to a house lit with candles and flashlights. I brought in the recliner to hold Shell and we tried to make life as 'normal' for her as we could. I could tell she felt worse, and it worried me.

Late that night her pump battery gave out and there was nothing we could do about it. She had been well hydrated up to this point, so we left it alone until the light of day.

The next morning, feeding Shelly became our primary concern. I foraged through boxes upstairs to find older medical supplies and located some feeding bags allowing for a manual drip. Tom took the pump to a friendly neighbor's house whose electricity was back on, and plugged it in to recharge.

Shelly grew more and more ill. She had begun to cough and it racked her body. If she was a person with veins, she would have been on IV antibiotics in a hospital. As it was, we could only keep her warm and I held her close to me as much as I could during the day. She weakened and my heart broke for her. Her sweetness increased as her life ebbed. I lived every moment in fear she would slip away.

The electricity was still off on Friday, but we had developed a system of sorts. Tom had been able to recharge Shell's battery with a converter device for his motorcycle battery, and we were making arrangements to get a back-up pump from Lexington.

The lights were back on for good by Saturday morn-

Ing so Shell's pump recharged during use.

Her skin color was paper-white, ashen around her lips and dark around her eyes. I was terrified for her. She was peaceful and beautiful and sleeping, but too weak to even let me pick her up and hold. It was the first time I could remember not rocking her. I sat by her bed and just watched her breathe.

Sunday morning, Tom and I went to separate church services, as usual, and we kept a close watch on the Bean. Her breathing sounded like pneumonia, very weak and listless. I got her up and held her, unable to bear another day without.

When I put her down and held her small sweet hands, she didn't pull away. I didn't know what to pray for, so I just prayed God would watch over all of us, that He would help us all through. This was Shelly and Shelly always bounced back. Always.

I slept poorly that night, worried about Shell's shallow breathing and occasional cough—I drifted into sleep, only to wake and find her silence frightening me to alertness, panicked she may die. My gut hurt with the stress of it, the agony of not knowing if there was anything else we could be doing.

This is how it ends for some people, I realized, but I didn't want it to end like this for Shelly. I didn't want her to be another ice storm statistic, added to the toll I was hearing about on the news.

When I could stand it no longer, I got up in the early hours and pulled her onto my lap, settling us on the recliner with her head heavy on my shoulder. The thought of not holding her was unbearable. What if she should die and I was across the room asleep? What if I was anywhere else, but holding her?

Once again, my Shell defied the odds. She got stronger and her temp went back to almost normal over the next few days. She played with her toys and grew restless with the mattress on the floor, threatening to get up and wander off when we weren't holding her. Finally, on Tuesday night her waterbed was all warmed up again, and she went back into it as if re-discovering an old friend.

For a long time her breathing was shallow, and there were times I needed to carry her in for her baths, holding her as she got in the tub, weak as a kitten. It dawned on me that her poor heart was giving out, fed by so few, thin and blocked veins for so long. How could her dear heart keep up?

I cried as I watched her, sweating and falling as she insisted on clearing the couch at night. She couldn't conceive of not doing it—every bit of her routine—her small life.

## ~ Forty-Nine ~

"How is Shelly doing?"
"I don't know. I think her heart is failing."
My own failing as I speak...

There is no practice for a day like today. There is only the one chance to get it right, and to that end, I feel I failed.

I didn't know what the day would look like, or feel like - the day Shell would die. I didn't know what frail meant in a life of fragility. I didn't know what her last heartbeats would sound like, or her last breaths would feel like.

There is no practicing this. It only happens once. And for it to happen to a child who survived so many close calls - who defied every prediction of doom - who rebounded every time rebounding seemed impossible, well... There are no practice shots for knowing when she would not.

My friend Linda came and spent the night before, a Thursday night. I'd not seen her in months, or heard from her in almost as long. Life had gotten complicated for her and she had pushed away, so I pulled to draw her back. I reminded her that we have 'karma' and she can't avoid it in the long run. Our families are joined somehow.

Shell had been growing weaker. I knew that. For several months I'd been giving her more and more support as she walked, and sometimes, even with my help, she would collapse, or swing out in a slow, turning spiral to the floor, smiling at herself when she did so.

"Silly me, I don't know why I did that!" Her laugh seemed to say.

I teased her as we got back in place, but my heart would lurch down with her and not get up as easily each time. I could see she was losing something she may not regain. My hold on her got increasingly supportive, until I was swooshing her from spot to spot.

Shell's color was poor, washed-out gray but it had been bad off and on for years. Her lips were blue by the time she got to bed, and she broke into a sweat with any exertion. She pinked back up within minutes of lying down and I would be relieved once again.

You would think I would insist on her resting more. I did insist, but Shell would have none of it. In the evenings, I would get her up. By then I would have changed myself into something comfortable, like sweats, filled her formula bag and pumped up her big ball. I'd change her into "day" clothes, brush her hair, and get my evening meal of banana and peanut butter, frozen blueberries and yogurt, all set up on a handy tray. I would help her out of bed and we'd bounce a long time on the ball, the TV going in the background, Tom in and out if he was around.

Sometimes when we finished bouncing I'd sign to her that we were going to sit on the recliner and other times I'd tell her she could sit with Papa. She paid close attention to whichever I signed, and if she knew Papa was home and around, she'd want it to be him.

"You go to Papa. Mama is going bye-bye. Mama wants a big hug!" I would sign before handing her off to Tom. I got long, hard hugs those nights.

With Tom she'd sit up, her back to him as the recliner stretched out. She'd laugh and make her 'Shell sounds' - we could never get enough of those. If she didn't feel well, she ground her teeth more - not our favorite Shelly sound.

The worse Shell felt, the more she wanted to sit with her Mama. With me, she cuddled. I can't express how lovely it was to cuddle with that child.

Several hours later we would start for bed.
I began by signing to her that we were going to get chang-

ed, and we'd exchange her shirt for another, or a night-gown. After more holding, I'd sign to her, "Now, you are going to bed!" and tap her left cheek three times (oh, child of routine!) and then kiss her cheek three times.

Helping her across the room, I quickly pulled a folding table to the end of the couch and place a wooden incense holder within reach. She would find it, and put it up on end to delicately balance before letting it fall to the floor. Then she would reach for the closest back cushion of the couch and hand it to me.

As Shelly grew weaker, I was 'allowed' to help her more and more. She checked the dogs stretched out on the floor or couch who were content to be part of the evening routine. If Laura was sitting on the couch and didn't move before Shell found her, she would feel her ears, pull her forward and give her a hug. The length and charm of the hug would depend on Shell's mood, though when she insisted Laura move, she meant *now*.

But the dogs received grace from the Bean, for whatever reason. She allowed them to stay where they were, and suffered me to put her hand on them for a petting.

At the other end of the couch Shell would reach to find the stuffed teddy bear my mother had left with us. After flipping it several times around in her hands and she would pass it to me over her head. On to the stuffed raccoon I must be sure to place in the right spot for similar treatment. Finally she would grab the second cushion and have me take it away. There - the couch chores were done.

On we went to the wooden medicine hutch. Over time I simplified this part, daily removing the boxes of tissues, wipes and gloves, leaving only the notebook I record her fluid measurements and one 60cc syringe. She would feel every inch of the counter top of the hutch for possible pens or forgotten papers and then would hand me the notebook over her shoulder before repeating her balancing act with the syringe.

Shell knew that if she opened the front cabinet door, she could pull an entire roll of paper towel from the dispenser inside. It was a joy I tried to cut short by moving quickly, but sometimes she happily rolled big wads onto the floor.

Finally, we reached the bed, her lips blue, showing a strain from her dear, hard-working heart. I approached her, and she would turn in a full circle and then push me away. I'd retreat, perhaps for enough time to begin getting her medicines ready, or fill her bag. At whatever point she decided enough was enough, she'd let me lift her into the waterbed.

Shell's last night on earth was different. I had taken her temp the day before and it registered 94.3—even for Shelly, that was low. Her sweating had increased of late, but this night she dripped enough to astound me. Still, she went through all her motions to get dressed, mostly sitting up in bed, as she had been doing more and more. I bounced with her gently on the ball, and she was glad to be with me. Linda, Tom, and I watched a movie.

When an hour of bouncing ended, I signed to Shell to let her know we would get in the chair. That's usually the time Tom offers to take her if I'm tired, and when he saw us moving, he said he'd be happy to hold her. I told him that I didn't want to let her go, and he knew why. Every moment I had with her was precious to me, and he didn't insist as he may have on a 'good' night.

We sat together until late. Midnight came and I would have given anything to convince her to skip her 'chores'. Her feisty spirit insisted on doing them, in spite of her failing body. I carried most of her weight across the room, and she barely touched the cushions and stuffed animals before letting me take them away.

Her legs were wobbly, and I thought she'd fall, so at the hutch I tried to support her weight as she tipped the syringe into perfect balance position. She shrugged me off with an exasperated sound, braced her shaky legs far apart and managed to tip the syringe perfectly. Seeming grateful for the fast track to bed, she sat up sweating as soon as she got changed.

She frightened me. She looked so fragile. But I have been scared before with Shell, many times. Just a week ago, Tom and I stayed watching her for a long time one night, afraid she was going, only to see her rally again. This girl didn't know how to die. How many times have I thought that? How many times has she proven that?

I stayed by her, mopping her forehead, changing her wet shirts. I kept kissing her head, breathing in her sweet, sweat smell that I couldn't get enough of - hugging her to me. She insisted on sitting up, and I wished for her old oversized pillow, long gone with the move, making a mental note to have Tom buy another one the next day.

Before she finally settled in, I signed to her for the last time.

If I had known it was to be our last signing together, I still would have said the same thing. I signed, "Mama wants a BIG hug!" She gave me a big hug, hard and long, and I as I write this, I can still feel her arms around my neck. I pray her touch is imprinted on me for every moment I need to draw it back again. Then I spoke with her as she sat there, her sweet head on a cushion. And I told her all the wrong things.

When our dear golden retriever Charlie died the month before, I could also see he was wearing out, and yet he faithfully stayed by my side, ever following me even outside to the end. I spoke with him then with his head on my lap, and told him all the 'right' things. I told him through my tears—that we knew he had to leave—that we would miss him dreadfully.

I told him we would be all right and praised him for

teaching Carl so well. I told him that Carl would now be there for us. You know, all that right stuff that theoretically heads them to the light without all the baggage. He died peacefully a couple of hours later.

But I didn't do this for my Shell. I cried and told her she did *not* have my permission to go—that I would miss her too much, and I couldn't bear to not see her and touch her. That she was irreplaceable, and my heart would break in two if she went. I said please—please don't leave... please don't go, Shell. I love you and I'm selfish and I don't want to face a day without my arms around you.

I said all the things I shouldn't say—every single word.

~ *Fifty* ~

*"One runs the risk of weeping a little, if one lets himself be tamed..."*
                              *(Le Petit Prince)*

The first thing Shell did on the day she died was to make me laugh. From our mattress on the floor, I looked up to see the couch cushion I'd given her stuck halfway through the rails of the waterbed. It was the place she got rid of things she no longer wanted. The cushion was too big, so it was stuck there. I wondered later at the energy she expended, precious heart energy she used up, working to clear her bed.

I did my usual things. Got her changed and as she felt cool, I put on the summer nightgown Tom's mom had made for her, added two cans of formula to her bag and enough pedialyte to almost fill it. I switched out her stomach fluid bag and measured the contents, setting it in the cabinet to use later. I kissed her and left to feed the dogs and have coffee with Linda.

I didn't know this day was like no other. I didn't know the moments I would wish back—at this point, I'd not made those moments, but I soon would, and there are no taking back moments in time. All the wishing and tears won't bring back the chance to be there for someone. We all just assume there will be more chances.

For years I'd worried about this very day, but I didn't know it was this day I'd always worried about. It was this day I'd thought of night after sleepless night, when she was ill, year after year from the time I met and first loved her. It was this day I wanted to be holding her. It was this day I most wanted to be there for her, feeling her angels surround her as they gathered her up to our Father. That she had to go, I knew. That I was not with her when she went, I couldn't bear thinking of.

Linda and I had a lot to catch up on, and I suggested a walk in our woods. Tom had left for Lexington early in the morning, and we expected him home soon, but I wanted some time alone with Linda. The ground would be wet, and she got her boots on while I went in to check on Shell. She was lying back on her pillow, about to fall asleep, still feeling cool. A toy board of gadget things lay across her lap, so I thought she may be cold. I pulled her dark red blanket out and put it over her, tucking the side between her knee and the wood of her bed.

She smiled at me. If the blanket was unacceptable to her, she would have tolerated it for a moment or two and it would have followed the path the cushion took earlier. But she smiled at me. That meant she was happy and more comfortable. I kissed her face, brushed her hair from her forehead, noting it was not freshly sweating. I told her I loved her and left her room.

How many times have I gone over that moment and the ones that followed? Why didn't I somehow know and pick her up? Cuddle her onto my lap in the chair, all out of her routine—hold her as she died...

How many times have I thought about that walk? When did it happen? Was it as we walked to the roses? When we stopped by Charlie's grave? When we followed the dogs down the path to the pond? Was it while we watched Carl swim or as we stepped through the woods?

Did the angels lift her as I lifted up that turtle, or when we climbed over the fallen tree in the path? Where was I? Where was I when I wasn't holding my little girl? Those moments haunt me. What did I have to say that was more important than sitting with Shell in silence? What was better to listen to than the rustling of angel's wings?

This must be the lost song of parents everywhere when a child dies. Our hearts will sing it in grief for the rest of our lives.

We must have been gone almost an hour and found Tom home, at the computer. We discussed lunch and started getting food out, but I said, "I'm going to check on the Bean."

How the world changes...

How is every step and word and thought recalled in slow motion? Walking into the darkened room, seeing something was 'off' and feeling the pool of dread well up from the floor I walked on - to the bed where Shell was lying tipped off to the left of her pillow.

Shell would never be off to the side of her pillow. It would be under her head, set straight behind her, or off the bed entirely. Shell believed in balance.

She must have sat up sometime after I left, but the blanket was still on her. She must have been sitting up and one beat of her heart was there, and the next never came. I lifted her head and pulled her toward me, onto the pillow. The beauty of her look, her perfect, sweet, peaceful face... it awed me. I whispered my very first thought to her, "What are you seeing, Shelly?"

Then that pool of dread reached my mind, and I called to her, hoping to catch her before she left and lead her back—I even pressed my hand to her chest, hoping her heart would flicker again for me and that she would just sigh, letting me know it was only a bad dream.

I knelt by her bed and stayed there—touching her face, talking quietly to her and crying. I could hear Tom and Linda in the next room as they started lunch. Two worlds that knew nothing of each other were coexisting, not just in the house, but in my mind. I wanted Tom, but didn't want him. If he came in, he could comfort me but he would also make it real, and I didn't want it to be real.

My limbs belonged to someone else. The only true thing was the feel of Shell's face. My hands cupped her cheeks, the touch of my fingers as they brushed her sweet lips, the softness of her skin on her small perfect hands—my Principessa.

## ~ Fifty One ~

*"It was wrong of you to come. You will suffer. I shall look as if I were dead; and that will not be true..."*
*I said nothing.*
*"You understand—it is too far. I cannot carry this body with me. It is too heavy."*
*I said nothing.*
*(Le Petit Prince)*

$\mathscr{I}$was alone with her for some time. Tom was used to me being gone longer than I thought when I checked on her. Perhaps she needed more food or to be changed. I don't know what he thought. When he did come to the door, I was still kneeling there.

I never asked him what his thoughts were at that moment—mine were distinctly odd. I thought how relieved I was that Tom and I were in love and solid.

If there had been any misunderstanding between us right then, it would have colored the moment—like having to step over things in a messy room to get to the window. What I knew about the man who came to the door was that he loved me, and would grieve with me, support me, comfort me and give me time.

Those moments were a blur. It could have been long or short, we may have spoken or not. I was too numb to record it. My mind went to the fierce protective areas of motherhood. This was not the first time I'd thought of Shelly's death, and some things were set in stone for me.

I would not let anyone come and take her away in a black bag as they did with our son Whitney. The image still haunts me.

I would let no one else prepare her body. She was my little girl and I would claim that honor one last time.

213

When I lost Vicky, I was too young to know that I might insist on such things. The years have taught me much about what I will allow, and what I can or cannot live with.

Tom stayed with Shell while I drew her bath. I thought he could use some time alone with her, and Linda had come in and left at some point. I poured warm water, shallow and filled with rose-scented bubbles. I put layers of towels on the floor in front of the tub and went back in for Shell. I don't know if Tom just read my face at the moment, or knew somewhere inside himself that I needed to do this alone.

I lifted her and carried her by myself past him to the bathroom, nudging the door shut behind us with my foot. I laid her on the towel, and marveled at her sweet, soft look, as if she had just fallen asleep and dreamt quietly.

I had not given her a bath in several days for a strange reason. The image in my mind - something from my past, perhaps a cheap plastic box or change purse—something sporting a tag saying, 'good for 1,000 openings.'

Lately, I had been quietly afraid that she had one of those tags invisibly about her- cautioning my heart that she only had so many baths, or so many walks, or so many exertions left.

Already in her past, I could look back at her standing on her head by the window, or twirling upside-down under her tire swing, or riding her tricycle in the yard. I knew those things were gone forever, used up and their last time unacknowledged. I didn't want to wear out one more moment of her life on something as foolish as an unnecessary bath, especially as I could see the normal joy they brought her being balanced by the terrible toll it took on her to even get to the tub. Instead, I chose bed-baths.

Taking off her nightgown, I blessed her arms and legs with my touch, feeling her fingers, taking care not to think beyond the moment and how holy it felt. I touched each scar covering her dear body, feeling places that had held IV

214

lines and remembered what it had hurt in me to see her go through every surgery. I traced the long marks crossing her her torso, for the gallbladder, the Nissen and more.

Finally, I lifted her into the tub's shallow water, unable to not remember how much she loved her baths, and the times she'd spent playing there. I washed her hair and body, being gentle with her face as I thought of her bath rituals—how everything had to be done in just the right order.

It was hard to lift Shell from the tub, and I was grateful for being strong, because I wanted to be alone with her. I dried her hair, put lotion on her body and then dressed her for the last time, putting on the first nightgown Tom's mother had made her- the warm one she loved so much.

By then my heart was so sore I didn't have the strength to lift her alone again. I called Tom to help and together we laid her back on the warm waterbed. At some point, Tom had made phone calls. I could feel myself almost growl at him, protective of who could know and what steps should be taken.

Tom and I are different in this aspect. He called the woman who works for the volunteer fire department to get the number for the coroner, for some reason wanting to be 'low key.' Perhaps he thought there would be some question about Shell's death in this new place where few people know her, or us. I would have just looked up the coroner's number in the phone book.

But before we called the coroner, I had questions, and wanted to make the first call to someone who loved Shelly, so I called Dr. Fulkerson's office and asked to speak with Nancy. I don't remember much of the call. Just that her voice was exactly what I needed, and that she suggested speaking with Scobee's Funeral home, where we had made pre-arrangements.

The man at Scobee's said we should get the local coroner, and if we wanted, either he or they would come for the body. I asked if we could drive her ourselves, which I planned to do anyway. He answered that it wasn't normally done, but there was nothing unlawful about it.

That was how we managed to get so many dear hours with Shell here at home. The coroner came after speaking with those at Dr.Fulkerson's, who had explained just how medically fragile her life was. They let him know they expected him to be kind to us.

I answered his questions as if through a visible fog in the room, and I had to try speaking clearly. Nothing I said seemed to make sense to me, and sometimes I thought I must have spoken when I did not. I was thinking he should go over and listen to her with a stethoscope because he didn't know her - he didn't know that Shelly didn't die easily. Perhaps he would listen to her and find that she had been quietly breathing all along - maybe she was only sleeping.

When he left, I sat with Shell, touching her clear perfect cheeks, savoring every moment with this body I would miss so much. Then, one by one, I named the people in her life that loved her, and kissed her softly for each of those who would never get that chance again, themselves.

I made the first of the phone calls that I would come to dread making— the calls to dispense bad and sad news, *mauvaise nouvelles* the French would say. I called Nathaniel and Isaiah, then Laura, and Julie, before everything became a blur to me.

God must have placed Linda's loving presence with us at this very time to lean on. Laura came as soon as she could, which gave her time with Shell at the house. She and Linda had made plans for a horseback riding session on Saturday, but the world had shifted and now they stayed at the house while Tom and I took Shell for the hour long ride to the funeral home.

I had found Shelly at 3:20 in the afternoon, and four hours later, we left with her in the Jeep. Tom drove while I sat with Shell in the back seat, her sweet head on my lap.

No one had rushed my time at home with her and I was grateful. My life was changing so drastically that if I was pushed, I felt that I would splinter irreparably into tiny shards of glass. Instinctively, Tom knew my state of mind and dealt patiently every step of the way.

I used the pillow from her bed, and her favorite blanket, I touched her still soft hands and face, and kept thinking the movement of the car would wake her and we would turn back for home. She had been lying on a warm waterbed since her warm bath, so she was still supple, her skin perfect and porcelain-like. She smelled of roses from her bath, hair soft under my fingers. I marveled at the goodness of God, allowing me to have this gift of time with this child who would be so hard to let go of.

The scripture, *"What is man, that thou art mindful of him, the son of man that thou doest care for him?"* must have been written for moments such as this.

There are people in your life who just show up - whether in person, on the phone, or in letters from their hearts.

Laura showed up. I called her- she came. She didn't hesitate to change her weekend plans, and didn't ask if I wanted or needed her here. She showed up because she knew I wanted and needed her here - relieving me of any guilt I might feel in asking for her.

At the funeral home, Nathaniel showed up. Tom and I needed him right then, and he walked in to fill the place only he could fill. He hugged. He listened. He sat close. He searched for missing people through avenues I wouldn't think of, like Facebook, or on-line searches. He called people I dreaded calling. He drove off to find people we couldn't reach by phone. He brought orange juice, crackers and a power bar, when he saw how puny I'd become so quickly.

He stood with us. He prayed with us. He didn't ask if he should do what he thought we needed, he just did it. He took on the responsibility of putting together the video with photos and music that I had envisioned. And so important to our hearts, he and Dana made sure to get our grandson, Alex, into our arms as soon as possible.

Also, that night at the funeral home, Julie showed up. She had been en route to a camping trip with her family when she got my message. Torn by responsibilities and direction, her husband took over the camping trip, no small feat with eight children. He left Julie, by her own insistence, at a gas station (babe in arms) to get picked up by her mother, and made it to the funeral home when I needed her most.

I needed her good sense when I had no sense at all. I needed the outlook from someone outside the immediate family. I needed her to see Shelly and stand in for all those who loved her and taught her and wouldn't get to come right away. I needed this friend who loved Shell so much to touch hearts with. She gently helped me with the write-up for the paper, and took responsibility for food after the service.

Isaiah showed up. And when he did, he never said if it was hard to leave work, or how long a ten-hour drive is. When I called him he said he loved me and he wished he was there to hug me. He listened when I spoke and listened when I couldn't speak. Then he and Stacia got in the car and showed up, completing our circle.

My brother, John, showed up. Shell was barely gone a day when John and his wife Linda showed up at our door, having driven the twelve hours from Pennsylvania. He is my brother John, and I needed him, and he came.

I can go on about those who showed up. Those who appeared with food at the door, with phone calls and emails—dear friends and family, changing plans and driving or flying to get here. Carol appeared, but I asked Jean not to come, knowing I would want her later when I just need to talk.

For many who couldn't physically get here, they promised to be with us in spirit, and they were.

## ~ *Fifty-Two* ~

*O*bituary:

Michelle T. never did what everyone expected. And what we expected on Friday afternoon was that she was napping, but in truth she was being gathered up in soul by angels who normally attended her on earth. That was all, from one heartbeat to the next, but what she left was her sweet spirit, and that will stay among us always.

For those of you who knew Shelly—her doctors and nurses, her intervenors and teachers, her social workers and friends, and mostly her family, well.... I don't have to tell you about her and what changes she wrought in all of us.

For all who didn't know Shelly, I'm sorry. She was almost unseen for years, yet cast a light to all who met her. She knew little of the world and its doings, but taught teachers and doctors, and inspired lives to change like few others have done in even a long lifetime. She died at age twenty-three but never lost a moment of innocence. She lived a perfect amount of time, and was sweet proof to all of us how much God loves us.

~ *Fifty-Three* ~

*~ Patti Kegley, Nurse ~*
*My heart aches for you Claire! I can't imagine how you are making it through these days and nights. I will say a prayer for you tonight... and many nights to come... because I am sure your heart is not done breaking.*

~ * ~

*I* promised myself yesterday that today would be different. Why is it the same?

But I had made that promise before I went to bed and cried for hours. I made that promise before I realized my dreams would be vivid and then disappear, making me search for them, trying to catch a tail end of one and bring it back to me.

It will be two weeks tomorrow that Shell died. I'm feeling the pressure from well-meaning people to 'get on with things'. I don't think they realize how much I've done - just being in large groups of people again, being outside in the evenings, even in the yard, putting one less-than-loved sweater of Shell's into the box for Goodwill. These things seem huge to me, and now people want me to come visit, go to weekend parties, travel.

My house is a mess. The other day I said I was going to clean the house. The next day I said, 'Okay—I'm going to clean the kitchen'. Today I said, 'Okay, I will at least get that one counter cleared off.' I can't seem to do it.

I stand up with resolve, pick up things like a normal person would, start a pan of dishwater or locate the broom. But the most ridiculous thing happens then.

I get lost.

I can't make even the simplest decision.

I find a nugget of dog food on the counter and stare at it, unsure of how to deal with anything that ambiguous. I don't actually form the words, even in my mind, but I am still trying to decide. Should I put it in with the other dog food under the cabinet? Should I feed it to a dog? And then get two other pieces from the cabinet for the other two dogs? Should I leave it for another time? Should I just knock it onto the floor and leave it to a lucky winner? That's how small my mind feels.

My dearest niece, Laura, called - from the goodness of her heart - and suggested I tweak my plans of getting in the car and driving twelve hours to visit Dad. Maybe I should wait one day and then go with her. Tom could come get me in a week. Or, plan B, which entailed flying, thus making it more scheduled... or....or.... And I'm standing there in my un-cleaned kitchen, almost in tears, without the words to connect a thought in my brain and wrap it around such a complicated idea. I end up in tears, on the couch with the phone and my poor niece having to extract herself from this call she made and likely wishes she didn't.

It took me (quite literally) hours to make banana bread last night. But it took me three days to get to the point of starting it. I have no energy, and feel sick with every moment crawling to the next, even as I wonder how the day flew past undone.

I scrabble to form a reasonable intention. Reasonably enough, considering the state of my house, I decide to put something away. In the process, I run across something of Shell's or a reminder—a picture, or a card. The moment holding the memory becomes lost time entirely, often leading right into another and another *lost-ness*. The next thing I know, I'm late feeding the dogs and birds and cats. I've let another day go by in a messy house.

I can't imagine what it must be like for those who unexpectedly lose a loved one. I'm saddened when I see yet another news reporter lift a microphone to the face of family members, fresh with loss, asking how they *feel*.

Surely, we are not so twisted that we want to hear

from a grandfather who accidentally ran over his grandson while backing up a car, or a mom who got crazy-busy bringing in groceries and starting supper and answering a phone to find that she'd left a child still in a car seat, or a dad unable to save his family in a fire. Mercy. Mercy.

People ask how I'm doing and my answer varies, but doesn't matter, because we're talking about different things entirely. They want to know if I'm, 'getting over it,' and I am thinking that I managed to not sit on Shell's ball, holding her pillow to my chest and breathing her in all day long. They want to know if I'm, 'getting out there,' and I am thinking about the dream of Shelly, waking me and making me smile. They want to know if I'm, 'making plans,' and I am holding onto a thread, desperately hoping I don't fall into irretrievable depression. Two entirely different conversations going on.

To move at all takes all I have sometimes.

*~ Bob Murray, Doctor ~*
*Shelly was such a special person in the world, that I carry her face with me over the years.*

I'm just beginning to get over the urge to walk up to complete strangers and blurt out that my little girl died. I have no idea why I'd even dream of doing such a thing, but it feels so immediate to me. Like a house is on fire and I must tell someone—like I just walked away from an accident as the sole survivor and have to get the word out—like I need them to know so they might realize life is not the same as it was before she died.

Somehow, every tiny molecule on my earth stopped but molecules are too small to be noticed and too important to be ignored.

This past Saturday, a missionary we work with came by the house. We were sitting out on the front porch, having coffee and banana bread at the round glass table. Very soon she asked about Shelly, who she'd never met, but had heard about. Finding it harder to speak than I would have thought, I told her of Shell's death and I was yet realizing there were people in our lives that we'd not told. She kindly said how sorry she was, and that it was understandable we were having trouble telling people.

I didn't know if I should say more. My whole being wanted to do nothing more than to tell her all about Shell, but maybe it wasn't okay to do.

I found it hard to talk, which makes people think you don't want to talk, which is not the case. I wanted to talk and cry and not feel bad about crying. I wanted to show every picture ever taken of Shell, and haul out her video with the music, and somehow bury the roots of Shelly's soul into this kind woman's heart, one more person to remember my Bean forever.

I settled on bringing out Shell's obituary and a small photo packet, watching Tom's face for indications I'd gone too far and was being inappropriate. He gave no such look, but I would have deferred to him in this case, as time and words still have not found their place in reality for me. I suppose I spoke about Shell for a few moments only, or maybe several minutes—but if an hour had passed by, I would not have realized it, and if I had said the same thing again and again, I may not have known that either.

Who would have thought this hole in my heart would be so big I could drop the real world into it without even touching it?

~ * ~

Yesterday, it was a month since Shell left. I met Tom downtown with some car warranty papers he needed and we went to the new Chinese restaurant for lunch.

Two women from church were there, who I've not seen in a long time and they hugged me and said they were sorry to hear about Shell. I know they'd never met her, but they were very kind, trying to say the right things and who knows what the "right" things are?

I stopped briefly at their table after they got their food, and tried some awkward chit-chat, knowing I should be trying to be good at this, this being around people. I'm still carrying Shell around on my sleeve, most likely visible to all.

I try to be light and breezy, but kindnesses bring tears to my eyes faster than anything and I'm afraid I place everyone I meet in a weird position, wondering if they should say something or not. I don't know what I'd tell them if they asked. I don't want them to feel uncomfortable, but often I want to do nothing but talk about Shelly...

When I got home from the restaurant, I let my excited dogs outside and got the mail from the box, spreading it on the porch table to read. There was a notice from a medical service provider for Shelly, determined to continue billing her long after she ceased needing their supplies, and a social security check, determined to continue paying her long after she ceased needing their money.

I saved two obvious cards for 'dessert'. One was from my friend Monica, a birthday card so well chosen that I read it aloud twice in enjoyment.

The second card was from Shelly's dear, dear Doctor Balint, at Columbus Children's Hospital. Finding a condolence card a month after Shell died was like drinking cool water in a desert—it gave me permission to sit out there and cry like I lost her afresh, which may sound awful, but is a balm.

It is so hard to try all the time to listen to conversations about this and that without my mind wandering back to my girl, trying not to look up at even complete strangers, eyes brimming with tears, as they talk on about other things.

This card tore my heart open, even as my fingers

tore open the envelope. Inside was the kind of card anyone who knew and loved Shell would send to her-one with a raised picture on the front- in this case lovely petals on a branch. I sat there for some time, not rushing to open it. Savoring thoughts of Shell and the endless kindness of Dr. Balint and Dr. Murray over the years, I touched its smooth paper.

Inside, she had written: *I hope you know how many people Shelly touched and how each of us who had the privilege of knowing both Shelly and you, even for short moments, are so incredibly blessed and are better for it. Please know my thoughts and prayers are with you. Despite the years, there are so many at Children's who have such vivid memories of Shelly, as if it was just a few months ago that she was here as a baby and little girl.*

The note helped heal my heart. A month since Shelly died, the cards are few now, of course—but even when they bring on a flood of tears and memories, I covet them coming.

As they dwindle in number I feel like I'm alone in grieving for her, left behind in a tidal flood on my own tiny island, unable and not willing to swim away from it. I can see a future of recriminating glances in the direction of my island, coming with guilt for not moving on, adhering to some politically correct master-clock for time allotted to grieving. I'm wondering how many other people are out there pretending, like I do, to be better than they are for the public moments, and are secretly wondering if they'll ever be normal again.

*~ Stacey Overturf, nurse ~*
*My friend Christine, who took care of Shelly, died in Oct. 2007 and I am so comforted that she is with Shelly. I'm sure I have no concept of heaven, but it does*

*make me feel better to know they are together. And... I was thinking, "Boy! Shelly must have so much to say and see!" What a glorious thought that she is whole again; not bound by her physical disabilities.*

## ~ Fifty-Four ~

There is no *easier* child to lose. Even after going through the deaths of three of my children, I cannot imagine losing a child who was expected to live. In that case, you mourn not just the loss of the child, but the probable future of that child - all the things like graduations, weddings, grandchildren - the loss would be compounded by imagining what could have been.

Losing a child like Shelly, has its own separate sorrow. It is true that I never pictured her getting married, or becoming an independent woman, or attaining a career choice—or even fixing a bologna sandwich. On the other hand, we were together every day, and everything we did revolve around each other, touching and moving through every situation and routine. Those of my children who have long life expectancies have moved on long ago to other arms and lives—Shell always stayed in mine.

Is the loss of a son or daughter in the military service easier, because they had knowingly put themselves in harm's way? Is the loss of a frustrating, hard to deal with child easier because some conflict may be gone? Of course not.

There is no *easier* child to lose.

~ * ~

"Well, now you can actually have a life," Someone said to me the other day.

I was speechless for a moment. I didn't know this man well and we were on the phone, which was good for him, because he couldn't see what a reaction I had to his comment.

I had a life.

Shell and I had a blessed life like few ever get to have.

~ * ~

I can't begin to know who I am. I guess this is also an empty nest syndrome. For the first time in twenty-eight years, we do not have a child in the house. A lot of people have difficulty dealing with that much alone, so maybe it's all part of why I feel like this. It keeps coming back to having worse days than others.

But I really don't feel like I know me at all. I was the Mama—the one who took care of someone. I was needed in a way that I am not anymore.

Now, I pass by Shell's room like someone with nothing to offer, haunting her bed still holding her toys and pillow, not sure I'll ever be able to make decisions about her things without falling apart. Maybe I should have already put her stuff away, but where is 'away'? We don't have a magic place of 'away'. Her toys make her sounds, her clothes linger with her essence, and her bed was her home. Where do I put them now? 'Away' isn't far enough away to stop missing her.

Yesterday, I thought I heard Shelly laugh. My heart stopped, even as I realized I had just caught the quick sound of our doves making their own kind of laughing noise. But just for that instant...

Instructions for Sorrow:
There are no instructions for sorrow. Some days are better than others, and some days are worse than others.

That's all.
Some days you can hardly get out of bed, not willing to leave the possibility of escaping into sleep.
Some days you can't wait to get out of bed after another long night, because too much thinking goes on while you should be sleeping. And too much thinking turns into

too much dreaming.

Other days you seem to be getting along pretty well, and the thought comes to your mind—perhaps the worst is over. And on a 'good' day like that, you may find yourself laughing about something among friends or family and feel a pang of guilt. Maybe it's from having forgotten your sorrow for a while. Maybe it's from laughing when crying still seems more appropriate.Maybe it's the thought of moving past the pain when you're not ready to move anywhere yet. Maybe it's because you're human and guilty feelings can come to humans for no good reason.

I needed to get Shelly's pump from the pole by her bed to return it to the home-health company.

I got it as fast as I could, pulling at the cord, unplugging it from behind the bed in the dark space without looking for spiders, twisting the holding mechanism with shaking fingers. I tried not to look at the bed, still strewn with her toys.

But a little purse caught my eye anyway, and I saw it still lying where she had put it—just so—where she would know where to find it when she woke from her nap.

*I can't go to Family Camp! I'm staying right here and not letting go of her things until I can think again - I'm going to grieve my heart out alone and no one can stop me.*

And I would have, too. But everyone kept up the concern of what was 'healthy' to do - mentally and physically.

When Shell died, I couldn't force myself to eat much, even with the constant urging of well-meaning people. But I didn't 'really have to eat'.

I was hardly going to starve, even if I didn't eat for days. I think it gives others something helpful to say. Perhaps there is something to the idea of keeping strength up, in a susceptible body. Maybe I'll use that line myself on a grieving friend someday.

But, healthy? It's not *healthy* to keep such sorrow?

I think you mean mentally healthy. And who has any idea what's mentally healthy for anyone else? There are still parts of Shelly my mind can't touch. I'm not ready. But as long as I look like I'm progressing, others are happy with me and around me.

I can't touch the sound of her voice for one thing. All those years I 'heard' her in a certain voice, and would use that voice for her when she gave certain looks or did certain things. But when it comes near my mind, I'm like a child who stops up her ears with her hands, 'na-na-na-na'.

I distract my mind to keep it from the torture of memory. Is that healthier than spending time with it, or giving myself time with it? I don't know. But I do know someday I'll face it, and be a mess, and then people will wonder when I'm ever going to 'get over' Shelly dying.

Last night we took a car up to Cincinnati for a missionary to use, which necessitated Tom and me driving separate vehicles and coming home together. It was late, and we'd not eaten so we stopped at a restaurant and had a lovely time together, talking and being in the moment—thinking of Family Camp, the missionary retreat we're starting, our dogs.

On the way out the door, we stopped at a revolving card rack and looked at the pictures of frogs, golden retrievers, and beaches in the sunset. I picked up the card with the angel before I realized exactly what it was-this angel wafting upward with a small child, a child the size of my little girl, being carried in her arms.

The child looked solid, like she needed to be carried, just like Shell was on those days before she died. Her arms were around the angel's neck, like hers had been around mine every day of her life. I put the card back and left crying as if she was a fresh loss, most of the way home. I kept thinking, 'You left without me! I would have taken you any-where, and this one time you left without me!'

It is hard to answer the question, "Are you doing better now?" As if losing someone and grieving are akin to having a bad flu.

## ~ *Fifty-Five* ~

I wonder if the dogs wonder
Where Shelly went.

I wonder if they wonder
If we realize she's gone.

I wonder if they wonder
Why we don't go get her.

I can't help them with this.

~ * ~

*I* should be better than this, and most of the time I'm pretty good. But many days catch me drifting along on a vast ocean of life, without any idea of how deep things are, or if and when I'll find a shore.
Shell had anchored me, and now I'm cut off from my anchor.

I ask God to hug her for me, to tell her I love her and miss her and to tell her I'm sorry I wasn't there when she left.

My cat Nebus is old, shutting down in fact. I think rigor mortis has actually set in and yet he's still up and walking, often purring. He shouldn't be breathing. His heart should have stopped sometime last month. He's old, he's blind, and he's probably having strokes. No pain, apparently, but definitely at his end.

I said on Saturday that if he made it until Monday, I'd take him to the vet to be put to sleep. He's afraid of riding in the car and I hate to have that be the last thing he does, so I'm hoping he'll drift off in his sleep... He does not.

Of course, he does not. He's a cat.

233

But today I woke up terribly depressed, missing Shelly so badly. I move through my morning routine, which is no routine at all, as if walking on the bottom of a murky pond—every step an effort, nothing clear, nothing easy. Nebus and I have a lot in common, I think...

I just can't kill the cat today.

I'll do it tomorrow...

I promise.

## ~ Fifty-Six ~

These are the days of our lives.

Today is November 13, 2009. Shell has been gone for five months and this would be her birthday. This is what parents who have lost a child do on birthdays—we struggle.

After all, I know Michelle is still alive, in another form and with God - so I want to celebrate her first birthday in Heaven. But I miss her here, on earth, and with me. I buy some of those shiny birthday balloons she loved, and I cry a lot. I'm glad to be alone today because, as I said, I cry a lot. But I want everyone else to remember her today too.

I'm grateful when I start up my computer this morning and see my sister-in-love Bonnie, has sent a joyful Happy Birthday card and a message telling me that she was thinking of us. There is a phone message from my Laura, singing Happy Birthday to let me know I'm not the only one knowing Shell is rejoicing elsewhere.

I want to say, 'Today is Shell's birthday.' Instead, do I say, 'Today would have been Shell's birthday?'

To me, she is still in the bed beside mine in the early waking of my mornings, between the times of dreams and reality. I almost think I'll get up and take care of her, listening for her sounds— the tap on a toy, the sloshing of the waterbed as she rocks herself, the laughing...

We placed a noise machine by our bed now, and so I hear the sounds of the woods all night long. These little machines are for drowning out other noises, but I use it to keep me from listening for my child.

So, Happy Birthday, Dearest Bean! Get the hug from our Lord that I'm sending to you. I love you and I hope you are so happy today. You are here in my heart, Principessa.

It has now been seven months and I've not taken

Shell's bed down. I'm not personally going to take it down. Tom told me months ago that when I was ready, he would do it for me. I told him I would be sure to be elsewhere--on another planet—on planet B 612, in fact—digging out an inactive volcano, just "in case".

Anywhere but at home—listening to the hose release the waterbed of the soft spot where she lay. Anywhere but home—listening to the boards being pulled apart to be burned as he promised me he'd do. Anywhere but at home.

We still sleep in the same room, but I put our twin mattress up on a frame to be off the floor. The room is crowded and when her waterbed is gone we will put a full sized bed in that corner and then be able to get to the door to the garage without rearranging furniture.

I wonder if I'll get used to a bigger bed, if Tom and I will lose each other in the night, not being aware of every roll-over and sigh. If it gets too bad, I'm sure we can return to our small bed again.

When I get up in the mornings I walk past Shell's bed and feel the height of the wood along my leg at the height I used to lean over her, where I would sit on the edge and touch her. I miss it; yet wonder if someday I will have to make myself call it to mind.

It frightens me I guess, that I may forget pieces of her. Maybe I'm not ready to take down the bed because I may wake up and go into the kitchen for coffee, and begin my day without even a thought of her.

The saying is, "Well, you'll always have your memories." But it's not really true. Always is a long time and even putting aside the chance of inheriting Alzheimer's, every memory seems to be mixed with so many other memories. It makes me wonder if they are actual memories at all.

After I write her book, I'll stop and let myself look at everything in the drawers under the bed—her blue sneakers, her yellow dress with red flowers, her sweatshirt say-

ing, "I love you" in sign language. I'll clear off the bed itself, where I have been putting her things—her floppy hats,
her binders and purses, her pillows. I'll check around the
water mattress for the kinds of things that got lost in
there—a sock, a pencil, a plastic hanger—parts of my heart.

~ * ~

It's April, and I'm cleaning out Shell's bed. A year
ago I was pulling these little tee shirts over her head, or on
cool evenings helping her tug on a sweatshirt.

I wasn't going to do this yet. I planned to wait until I
was ready, but I can see it will not be easy to do, even
years from now. And I know Tom deserves a 'real' bed after twenty-two years of sharing a single mattress. He
waited without complaint for me to do this when I could.

We have a full sized mattress and box springs in the
garage, given by a friend. The metal frame under our single
bed will expand to hold it, and we'll not need more. The
roominess alone will be a luxury. But, aside from knowing it
would be so hard to do, I stayed so unmotivated about it
all.

So I researched bed netting. I've always loved the
thought of sleeping under a canopy of netting. I found a
lovely white one to hang from the ceiling, and ordered it
over the internet. By a stroke of good fortune it showed up
just before Tom got home yesterday, so I could hide it. I
felt guilty for spending the money on it, though it really
wasn't much. It will be the cost of his getting a big bed.

I also changed my mind about Shelly's bed. I asked
Tom earlier to burn it, as I couldn't bear the thought of it
lying in a trash heap somewhere. With the coming of a new
spring I decided instead to use the solid wooden frame of
the waterbed as a place to grow herbs and perhaps some
'Forget-me-not' flowers.

There is a perfect sunny south-side spot in the back
yard for it, and I will be happy to watch living things grow-
Ing in there all summer. Perhaps, someday, Tom's dream of

237

a small greenhouse will be built around it.

I'm steadily working my way through a box of tissue, as I carefully take each item from the drawers under the waterbed. I inhale the breath of my Shell from the familiar clothes hidden away since she died.

I make piles. Some new things I don't care about, even sporting store tags in many cases, all go in the pile for *Goodwill*, easy enough. But the larger pile is what I treasure and can only put in a big box I found. It will stay here in the room until I can bear to put it in a closet for storage.

I unfold and hold against my cheek her red sweatshirt reading *Columbus Children's Hospital* and remember the day we left there after a week, when the weather changed to bitter cold, so I ran to buy it in the gift shop, several sizes too big.

I keep the purple sweatshirt that she painted in school of a bunny, Shell's feet and toes, having made the ears, her handprints making the whiskers, Easter-1996.

One after another, smoothed over with my hands, folded with love, I make myself continue through her life of clothes. When I take out her shirts I'm a blubbering mess. I know some of them are presentable enough to send to Goodwill, but I just can't. I just won't. Kids all over the world will have to get their clothes elsewhere, because I can't bear the thought of anyone else in these.

I don't care if it sounds selfish. It is enough for me to do right now.

So, I'm not moving on. That implies leaving Shell behind and I'd never leave her behind. Instead, I'm moving toward her. She's moved on, and I'm following in the best way I can, feeling my way along until I'm with her again.

I always begged God to let her go first, so she would never be lost without me, sick and confused. I know so many parents of fragile children who have begged Him for the same. I am the one who is lost, missing her, and that's easier, somehow, to bear.

How many times parents wish they could take the pain from their children onto themselves? He granted me that, and I now find myself far enough from the epicenter of grieving to be grateful.

Shell's days of pain are over forever--her weakness, her labored breathing, her fragility—all over now. I look to the stars and know her laughter is not gone. Her beautiful soul survives, without the trials. I would not wish her back here on earth again, no matter how my arms ache for her.

I will spend years with you when there are no years— and time with you when there is no such thing as time—I will only miss you here for a while. A touch of a moment in unspeakable eternity...

I'm coming Beanie, my Principessa. Wait for me.

Yesterday was a year
Since Shell left us for heaven.
Today God sent us a
Feisty, red-headed grandchild,
Norah Kate.
He is good.
He is always and blessedly good.

~ *End* ~

Made in the USA
Charleston, SC
14 January 2015